BARNES & NOBLE BASICS™

personal budgeting

by Barbara Wagner

BARNES
& NOBLE
BOOKS
NEW YORK

For information, contact:
Silver Lining Books
122 Fifth Avenue
New York, NY 10011
212-633-4000

Other titles in the **Barnes & Noble Basics**™ series:
Barnes & Noble Basics *Using Your PC*
Barnes & Noble Basics *Wine*
Barnes & Noble Basics *In the Kitchen*
Barnes & Noble Basics *Getting in Shape*
Barnes & Noble Basics *Saving Money*
Barnes & Noble Basics *Getting a Job*
Barnes & Noble Basics *Using the Internet*
Barnes & Noble Basics *Retiring*
Barnes & Noble Basics *Using Your Digital Camera*
Barnes & Noble Basics *Getting Married*
Barnes & Noble Basics *Grilling*
Barnes & Noble Basics *Giving a Presentation*
Barnes & Noble Basics *Buying a House*
Barnes & Noble Basics *Volunteering*
Barnes & Noble Basics *Getting a Grant*
Barnes & Noble Basics *Getting into College*
Barnes & Noble Basics *Golf*
Barnes & Noble Basics *Your Job Interview*
Barnes & Noble Basics *Résumés and Cover Letters*
Barnes & Noble Basics *Starting a Business*

introduction

"I just don't get it. I bring home a decent paycheck, but I always run out of money before the end of the month," complained my friend Jim. "I've even had to use my credit card to buy groceries. How do I get out of this financial mess?"

How indeed! All you need are these three little words: a personal budget. And that's where **Barnes & Noble Basics** *Personal Budgeting* comes in. Inside these very helpful pages, you'll find everything you need to create a budget you can live with. First, use the user-friendly worksheets to track your expenses and calculate your net worth. Next, find your spending leaks. And finally, learn how to set reasonable spending guidelines and savings goals. We'll even show you how to invest your savings wisely, so that they'll build even more wealth for you. Along the way, you'll also get tons of money-saving tips.

Take the first step toward financial freedom by turning the page. You'll soon see how easy it is to get your finances back on track.

Barb Chintz
Editorial Director, the **Barnes & Noble Basics**™ series

table of contents

Chapter 7   Budget Stretchers

Chapter 8   Managing Your Debt

Chapter 9   Making the Most of Savings

Getting Started

CHAPTER 1

"Believe it or not, all you need is a budget."

budgeting benefits

What a budget can do for you

The mortgage. Your retirement. Groceries. Credit card bills. Home renovations. Clothes. College tuition. Holiday gifts. And on and on. So many demands competing for your hard-earned money can make your head spin—and leave your wallet empty.

But don't despair. Believe it or not, all you need is a **budget**: a simple financial plan that will help you make the most of your money. No matter how many bills you have or how much—or little—money you earn, a budget can help you make smarter spending decisions and stay out of debt. It can also help you set realistic financial goals and calculate the cost and time frame for your goals. In short, a budget can put your financial life in order.

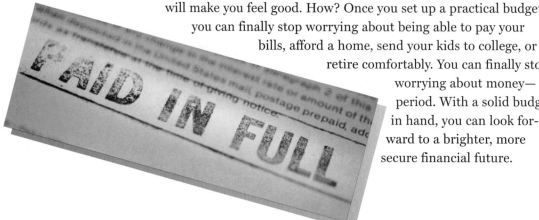

What's more, a budget will affect more than just your finances. It will make you feel good. How? Once you set up a practical budget, you can finally stop worrying about being able to pay your bills, afford a home, send your kids to college, or retire comfortably. You can finally stop worrying about money—period. With a solid budget in hand, you can look forward to a brighter, more secure financial future.

20 really good reasons to set up a budget

A budget will help you:

1. Stop living from paycheck to paycheck
2. Get out of debt
3. Stay out of debt
4. Get a grip on your spending
5. Curb impulse purchases
6. Find ways to cut costs
7. Build an emergency cash fund
8. Set and prioritize financial goals
9. Start a savings program
10. Be a smarter consumer
11. Retire early
12. Learn to live within your means, so that you may be able to accept a lower-paying, but more rewarding career
13. Live on less money, so that you may not have to work a second job and can then spend more time with your family
14. Pay your bills on time
15. Meet your family's changing financial needs
16. Reduce stress associated with saving for big expenses
17. Distinguish between "needs" and "wants"
18. Stop making ends meet with a credit card
19. Keep some "mad money" to splurge with
20. Sleep at night without worrying about your bills

the right attitude

Put yourself in a money-saving state of mind

What's the secret to setting up a successful budget? Grab a pencil and some paper—and get started. That's it. The obstacle that keeps most nonbudgeting folks at bay is simple procrastination. Many people, especially those who seem to need a budget most, just can't find the time or energy to start tracking their spending and forecasting their expenses.

Having the proper mindset about budgeting can help you get over this procrastination hump. Don't think of a budget as a straightjacket; instead, consider the reasons a budget is good for you. For example: A budget will improve your financial security. It will help you pay down your debt. It will help you curb impulse spending. It will also help you learn how to set— and reach—realistic financial goals. In short, it can do wonders to improve the quality of your life.

Having the right mindset also means believing that drawing up and maintaining a budget is not beyond your capabilities. Forget the advanced mathematical calculations that you think are required. You'll need to do elementary math—and that's it. Plus, there are many resources out there that can help, including money software, Web sites, and financial professionals. So remember: Help is there if you need it.

One wonderful thing about budgeting is that it gets easier over time. The longer you use a budget, the more skilled you'll become and the less time you'll need to manage it. The longer you use a budget, the more likely it is you will keep at it. The longer you use a budget, the more you'll wonder how you ever survived without it. The bottom line: Once you get started, a budget is easy. So . . . let's get started.

Who needs a budget?

To test your budget know-how, answer "yes" or "no" to the following questions:

- When your bills arrive, are you ever surprised at how much money you spent?

- At the end of a pay period, do you ever wonder where your paycheck went?

- Do you buy on impulse instead of planning your purchases?

- Do you live from paycheck to paycheck?

- Do you feel that you just can't get ahead financially?

- Do you avoid talking to your spouse about money?

- Do you think that being in debt is okay?

- Are you worried about your financial security?

- Are you distressed about the size of your credit card debt?

- Do you wish you had a filing system for your bills?

Answer key: If you answered yes to any of the above questions, you're not alone. Like you, many folks put off any attempt at budgeting because a) they think anything that has to do with money is too complicated; b) they're too busy working overtime to pay off that pile of bills; c) their father, mother, brother, sister, husband, wife, or best friend handles their money for them; or d) all of the above. The good news? You can turn these yes answers into no's—and manage your money better.

the right information

Take your little notebook everywhere for three months

Even if this is your first attempt to budget, you've probably heard about the spending diary. Before you can create a budget, you need to figure out where your money is going. That's where a spending diary comes in. Get a little notebook and bring it with you everywhere. Immediately jot down every cent that you spend (whether by cash, credit card, debit card, or check). Well, okay, maybe you won't always be able to do it immediately, but you do need to record this information in chronological spending order. That way, you'll be more conscious of what you're spending.

Keep this financial diary for at least one month, but preferably three. (One month may include atypical expenses; three months will provide a more realistic snapshot of your spending patterns.) And include everything you buy—even that daily cup of latte. If you use an ATM, don't simply jot down the amount withdrawn. Instead, write down exactly what you bought with the cash. You can't put together a budget, in fact, until you've collected this information. The good news: Once you get into the notebook habit, you'll be able to write down your expenses in just a few minutes each day. What's more, after a few weeks of watching what you're spending, you'll probably start spending less, because you'll be forced to see just how much money you spent on frivolous things every week.

A sample entry from your spending diary

Friday, May 15

coffee	$2.50
newspaper	$1.25
bus fare (to work)	$2.50
lunch	$5.00
shampoo & razor blades	$7.50
candy bar	$.75
bus fare (home)	$2.50
take-out Chinese food	$18.00
Girl Scout cookies from kid next door	$6.00
Suzie's class trip	$15.00
video rental late fee	$3.50

The right tools

Remember the first day back at school after summer vacation? Crisp notebook pages that crinkled when you turned them. Pencils sharpened to perfect points. You couldn't wait to use all that bright, new stuff. That first-day-of-school excitement is exactly the attitude you want to bring to the budgeting table. To get started, you'll need these supplies:

A small notebook. This is the most important item on this list because it will help you track your current spending. (See the page at left for details.) Buy one for each member of your family. Be sure it has lined pages and is small enough to fit in a purse, briefcase, or shirt pocket. You'll want to carry it everywhere!

Sharpened pencils. When drawing up a budget, you'll use up a lot of lead calculating—and recalculating—your expenses, income, and other figures. To keep your notes neat and legible, stick to pencils. It's harder to make changes when the numbers are written in ink. Don't forget to keep an eraser on hand, too.

A filing system. You don't need an elaborate system for organizing your paperwork, just a convenient place to store your bills and receipts, such as file folders or shoeboxes. You can keep incoming bills in one file, last year's paid bills in another, and current receipts in a third. The less complicated your system, the more likely you are to maintain it.

A calculator. Forget those fancy, expensive models that compute square roots and complex logarithms. When budgeting, you have to add, subtract, multiply, and divide—and that's it. Find a calculator that performs these basic functions and is easy to use. If you have trouble seeing small figures, get one with extra-large buttons. A solar powered model might also be a good choice because it doesn't need batteries.

the right stuff

**Where to find
the numbers
you'll need**

With your spending diary underway, the next thing you need to do is start organizing all your bills and receipts. We'll use these to come up with a realistic picture of your spending in Chapter 3. Create a handy filing system for the following:

- **Pay stubs for you (and your spouse, if applicable)** showing the amount of your take-home pay.

- **Your most recent tax return** provides income information. And, if you itemize, it shows the amounts spent on certain expenses, such as medical bills.

- **Your checkbook register for the past year** contains information about how much you spent on what. Your register will be most useful if you make a lot of purchases by check, clearly note the amount and item purchased, and balance it regularly.

- **Your credit card statements for the past year** offer a detailed record of how much you spent on clothes, furniture, groceries, and more.

- **ATM, debit card, and miscellaneous receipts** provide lots of information, especially about cash purchases. Even if you pay for things in cash, make sure to get a receipt so you can list everything in your spending diary (see page 12).

- **Your bank statements for the past year** will also show you what you paid for by check. Bank statements often include canceled checks or miniature photos of canceled checks; they also document ATM withdrawals and any electronic payments.

- **Your monthly mortgage statements** include information about payments made on your home mortgage, second mortgage, home equity loan, and real estate taxes. You'll probably find these amounts in your checkbook register, too—unless you don't note the payees.

- **Interest statements** from any savings accounts, stocks, bonds, or other investments you may have.

ASK THE EXPERTS

I've tried to keep track of my expenses in the past, but I always seem to get overwhelmed. Any tips?

Start small. Tracking your expenses can indeed be overwhelming. But there's no reason to panic. You won't be able to track every single cup of coffee you buy or every newspaper you purchase. But don't let that keep you from trying. First, start collecting receipts from every purchase you make. Record these expenditures in your spending diary. As you write checks, make sure to write down the date, check number, payee, amount, and description of each. Then once or twice a month, sit down with your receipts, your diary, your check register, and your credit card statements to track what you've spent. If you're PC literate, consider compiling these in personal finance software (like Quicken). See pages 16-17.

How long should I hold on to receipts and records?

You should keep copies of your tax returns for seven years. The statute of limitations for tax audits is generally three years, but the IRS can actually call you up to six years after you filed if they think you underpaid. And there is no statute of limitations on outright fraud. Bank statements should, likewise, be kept for seven years (for tax purposes). You can toss ATM receipts, though, as soon as you receive a bank statement documenting those transactions. Credit card statements should be kept for an entire year. Paycheck stubs should be kept until you've received a W-2 form for that year. And general household bills and receipts can be discarded after you've noted the amounts in your budget worksheet, unless any of these expenses are itemized on your tax return. Then you should file those papers with your tax returns.

money software

Your computer can help you budget

If you're comfortable using a computer, consider tracking your expenses with **personal finance software**. Three of the most popular programs are Microsoft Money, Quicken, and Mvelopes. These and other personal finance software programs are available at most computer stores for both PC and Mac users for under $75.

What can they do for you? Plenty. They'll help you set up a tailor-made system to organize your personal finances, investments, and tax records. If you bank online (see page 20), most software will also let you transfer information about your banking transactions directly to your budget. For example, you can set up the software so that if you write a check for $45 to your dry cleaner on May 10, this will show up in your dry-cleaning expense category. Some software even lets you write checks, print checks, or, if you prefer, send payments online. Another nice feature: The software can create a schedule of payments for loans and monthly credit card bills, alert you to dates when payments are due, and, in some cases, even let you pay them online.

Quicken

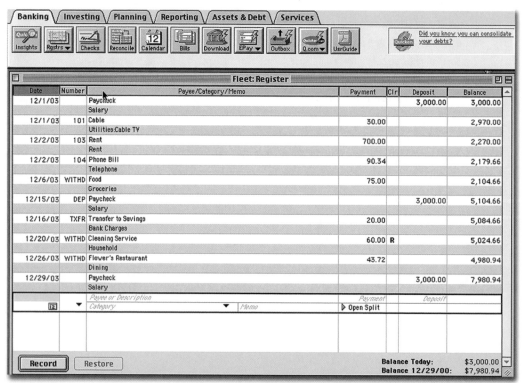

Date	Number	Payee/Category/Memo	Payment	Clr	Deposit	Balance
12/1/03		Paycheck / Salary			3,000.00	3,000.00
12/1/03	101	Cable / Utilities:Cable TV	30.00			2,970.00
12/2/03	103	Rent / Rent	700.00			2,270.00
12/2/03	104	Phone Bill / Telephone	90.34			2,179.66
12/6/03	WITHD	Food / Groceries	75.00			2,104.66
12/15/03	DEP	Paycheck / Salary			3,000.00	5,104.66
12/16/03	TXFR	Transfer to Savings / Bank Charges	20.00			5,084.66
12/20/03	WITHD	Cleaning Service / Household	60.00	R		5,024.66
12/26/03	WITHD	Flower's Restaurant / Dining	43.72			4,980.94
12/29/03		Paycheck / Salary			3,000.00	7,980.94

Balance Today: $3,000.00
Balance 12/29/00: $7,980.94

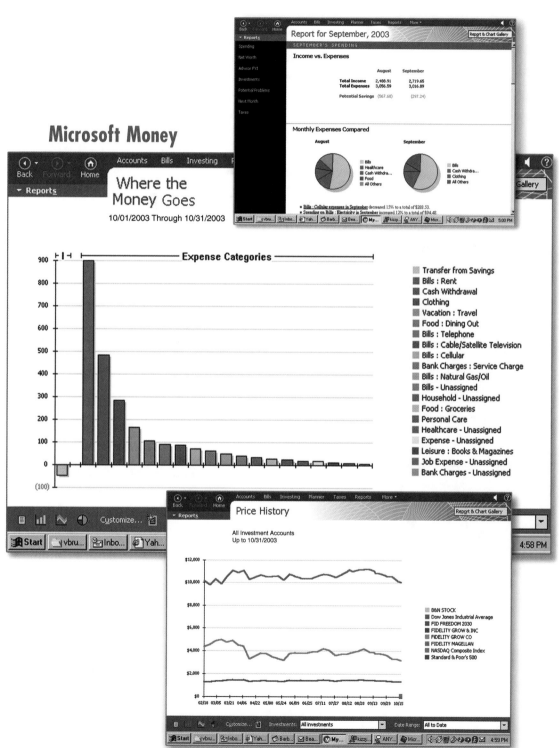

Microsoft Money

Report for September, 2003

SEPTEMBER'S SPENDING

Income vs. Expenses

	August	September
Total Income	2,488.91	2,719.65
Total Expenses	3,056.59	3,016.89
Potential Savings	(567.68)	(297.24)

Monthly Expenses Compared

August — Bills, Healthcare, Cash Withdra..., Food, All Others

September — Bills, Cash Withdra..., Clothing, All Others

- Bills : Cellular expenses in September decreased 1.5% to a total of $288.53.
- Spending on Bills : Electricity in September increased 1.2% to a total of $94.48.

Where the Money Goes

10/01/2003 Through 10/31/2003

Expense Categories

- Transfer from Savings
- Bills : Rent
- Cash Withdrawal
- Clothing
- Vacation : Travel
- Food : Dining Out
- Bills : Telephone
- Bills : Cable/Satellite Television
- Bills : Cellular
- Bank Charges : Service Charge
- Bills : Natural Gas/Oil
- Bills - Unassigned
- Household - Unassigned
- Food : Groceries
- Personal Care
- Healthcare - Unassigned
- Expense - Unassigned
- Leisure : Books & Magazines
- Job Expense - Unassigned
- Bank Charges - Unassigned

Price History

All Investment Accounts
Up to 10/31/2003

- B&N STOCK
- Dow Jones Industrial Average
- FID FREEDOM 2030
- FIDELITY GROW & INC
- FIDELITY GROW CO
- FIDELITY MAGELLAN
- NASDAQ Composite Index
- Standard & Poor's 500

using the Internet

Many of your budgeting questions can be answered online

The Web is home to a massive amount of information on managing your finances. You'll find many sites offering tried-and-true savings tips, online budgeting worksheets, and experts' columns. In addition, you can compare notes and insights with others via bulletin boards, chat rooms, and forums. There is probably no better way to overcome your budgeting anxieties than by sharing them with others. (Just be careful about posting sensitive personal financial information that others can read.)

Here are some budgeting Web sites worth checking out:

- **www.personal-budget-planning-saving-money.com** Learn how to calculate your net worth, find and stop spending leaks, get out of financial trouble, and practice self-control.

- **www.savingsecrets.com** Home to more than 50 articles on saving money and five electronic books you can order. You can also sign up for a free biweekly, personalized budgeting e-zine and take advantage of extensive tips, updated monthly.

- **www.tuliptreepress.com** This informative site covers myths about budgeting and getting motivated, and includes targeted advice for newlyweds and women.

- **www.in2m.com** The personal online budgeting system from Mvelopes. For a low monthly fee, you can use the innovative "envelope" system to track and control your spending, link your budget to your bank account, pay bills online, and get unlimited expert advice by phone.

ASK THE  EXPERTS

I want to learn more about debt reduction, retirement planning, and other financial topics. How do I find Web sites that address these issues?

Search engines, such as Excite or Yahoo!, look through the whole Web and produce a list of sites related to key words you plug in—for example, debt reduction. But thanks to the popularity of financial information, many of these search engines now offer mini search engines just for personal finance and money. Check out the financial sections of these popular search engines:

Excite—**www.money.excite.com**

Yahoo!—**www.finance.yahoo.com**

Microsoft—**www.moneycentral.msn.com**

Netscape—**http://moneynetscape.ccn.com**

Can I use the Internet to find a credit card with a lower interest rate?

Yes. Financial Web sites make it easy to find competitive interest rates. Two sites that compile a comprehensive range of the best credit card deals are **www.bankrate.com** and **www.bestrate.com**.

What are these "calculators" I see on some sites?

Many Web sites have free financial calculators that can help you figure out things such as how much you need to save every year to meet your retirement goals or how long it will take you to pay off your credit cards. You simply plug your financial information into the calculator and voilà, the answers are revealed. You can find several useful calculators at **www.bloomberg.com**, **www.financenter.com**, and **www.kiplinger.com**. Also take a look at **www.usatoday.com/money**.

banking online

View transactions with a click of your mouse

One way to streamline the budgeting process is to sign up for online banking. When you bank online, you'll be able to review your account transactions 24 hours a day—and your checkbook is balanced automatically. Just think: No more waiting for your account statement to arrive in the mail or bouncing checks because you have miscalculated how much is in your account.

Online services vary somewhat by bank. Some, for example, will waive all fees if you agree to have your paycheck deposited directly into your account, make a certain number of payments online instead of using checks, or bank only through ATM machines. See how various banks stack up by visiting **www.cyberinvest.com**. Click on the site's Banking Center and then choose "The Guide to Online Banks."

What about security? Banks take online security very seriously, especially since even the smallest glitch can severely damage customer confidence. For starters, banks have fire walls (computer programs that act as gatekeepers so only authorized people can get in). When you sign up for online banking, you get your own password and Personal Identification Number (PIN). Passwords make sure you are who you claim to be when you log in, while PIN codes verify and confirm each banking transaction you perform. And thanks to encryption (a process used to convert data into unrecognizable numbers), none of your personal information can be read over the Internet by unauthorized people.

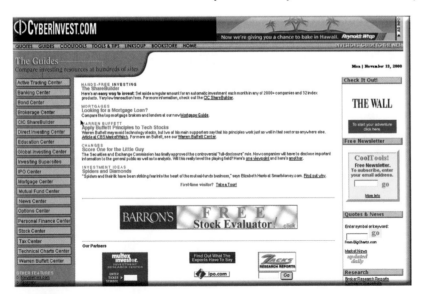

ASK THE  EXPERTS

How can I get cash if I bank online?

If only your computer could magically turn into an ATM! Alas, to get money, you must resort to old-fashioned tactics such as going to a real bank or withdrawing from an ATM machine. When you withdraw money from an ATM machine, the amount is posted immediately to your online account.

How can I pay bills online?

You can do this by having funds electronically transferred from your account to the account of your creditor. Usually the fee for this transaction is included in your monthly online banking service charge. First, you enter the creditor's name, address, and your account number with them. Then, you enter the amount of the payment and with a few clicks of your mouse, the money is on its way!

You can also set up your online account to automatically pay certain bills every month. For example, if your monthly cable bill is always $49.95 and is always due on the 15th of every month, you can arrange to have that amount automatically paid to the cable company each month by the due date. If you set up an automatic bill payment method with your bank, there is usually a small monthly fee.

To make life even easier, you can also set up electronic fund transfers with your creditors. This is much like having direct deposit for your paycheck, only in this case you are having money taken out of, rather than put into, your account each month to pay creditors. The amount varies depending on your bill. Not only does this save you a stamp and the time of writing a check, but it also ensures that your bills are paid by the due date. Contact your creditors and ask them to mail or fax you an electronic transfer agreement form. Usually, you can also arrange for electronic fund transfers at the creditor's Web site. In many cases, this service is free.

a family affair

If you are on your own, budgeting is a bit easier because you only have yourself to account for. But if you have a partner and/or children, it's important to get them involved in the budgeting plan, or else they'll simply continue old spending habits. That will make it difficult—if not downright impossible—to keep track of the amount your family spends.

To get everyone in on your budget plans, call a family meeting. Fix a time and place, preferably one without distractions. Explain what a budget is, why your family needs one, and how everyone will benefit. Then ask everyone about their financial needs and goals. To make the budget work, you all need to set and prioritize your financial goals, then work together to achieve them. (Learn more about setting goals in Chapter 5.)

Make it clear that while a budget certainly isn't meant to be a punishment, some new spending restrictions will apply. One bright

spot: Constraints aren't carved in stone. You can tweak your budget from one month to the next until it "feels" right.

Plan to reconvene every month to look at what worked and what didn't. Did you really spend just $75 per week on groceries, or was that number unrealistic? How did the brown-bag lunches work out? Brainstorm ways that you can raise money (a part-time job? a garage sale?) or cut expenses further (by carpooling to work, for example).

Finally, consider setting up a reward system. After you save a certain amount of money or stick to your budget for three straight months, celebrate with, say, a day at the beach. (Just make sure to pack your own lunch, and skip the expensive deli meal!)

Pick a money maven

While everyone should be involved in your family's finances, many families find it more practical for one person to handle the day-to-day money management. This "designated driver" pays the bills, balances the checkbook, and makes sure the taxes get filed by April 15. In many households, the money person either likes working with numbers or is simply best at it.

Some couples trade off these duties. This year, one partner handles the money; next year, the other partner does. Other families break the job in half, because when it comes to finances, there's a lot to be done—even within one family. One partner manages the day-to-day stuff like paying bills and balancing the checkbook, while the other oversees long-range issues like investing for retirement or college tuition. Other couples institute a "checks and balances" system: One partner pays the bills and the other partner balances the checkbook. Once you decide how these responsibilities will be assigned, make a list of all the financial duties and make sure everyone is clear on who is charged with doing what.

No matter what system you and your family choose, it's crucial for the long-term security of your family that both partners understand the family's finances. We all imagine that our spouses will be with us forever, keeping tabs on that errant checking account. But death and divorce are a fact of life. One day you may suddenly find yourself forced to do it by yourself. That's why, no matter who's paying the bills today, it's essential to make sure that you and your spouse both know:

- what your expenses are

- how much money you earn

- what your assets are and how much they are worth

- how to pay bills

- how to withdraw from and deposit money into your accounts

- how your filing system works

- where your important papers are

using a financial planner

Don't be afraid to seek some professional help

When faced with an important decision, many people seek the advice of a professional. For legal issues, they consult a lawyer; for medical issues, they visit a doctor. And for money issues? They go to a **financial planner**.

Financial planners can advise you on everything from drawing up a budget to getting out of debt to saving for retirement or college tuition. They can tell you whether or not your financial goals are reachable and if your savings plan is on the right course. And, if you are not comfortable devising your own investment strategy, they can also help you map out a plan, suggest the best routes to reach your goals, and coordinate all you need to get there.

Unlike most other professions, however, the financial planning industry is largely unregulated. Virtually anyone can hang out a shingle and call himself a financial planner. That's why it's important to check out a planner's credentials before you sign up. (See page 25.)

Another way to distinguish among planners is to find out how they're paid. Most people new to budgeting start off by hiring the services of a fee-only advisor who charges an hourly rate. Other **fee-only planners** charge a flat fee or charge a percentage of the assets they manage for their clients. The financial advice of a fee-only planner is objective. They may recommend you buy certain investments, but they will never earn a commission for selling you a particular stock or mutual fund.

Commission-based planners, on the other hand, do not charge directly for their advice. Instead, they earn a commission if you invest money through them in a stock, mutual fund, or other investment. While their budgeting advice may be fine, be wary if they push you to invest in certain stocks or funds.

ASK THE  EXPERTS

What can I expect if I work with a financial planner?

You can expect to have several meetings. Some will charge by the hour (especially those who are helping you through a particular rough patch), others will charge a set fee for a certain number of meetings—such as four or five—or for services provided over a period of time, such as six months. At the first meeting, the planner may ask what prompted your visit. If you want to address an emergency (such as out-of-control debt), the planner should focus on that issue right away. He or she will ask questions about your debt problems and your finances in general. If you want a complete fiscal examination, the planner may ask you to bring your tax returns, investment statements, and other financial documents on your second visit. Why? This information will help the planner get an overview of your financial situation. The planner will ask about your short- and long-term goals. When do you plan to retire, for instance? Do you expect to pay for your children's college tuition? Then, over the next visit or two, the planner will recommend some of the best ways to get you where you want to go. This might mean helping you draw up a budget, suggesting changes in your investment strategy, or finding smarter ways to borrow money.

Who's who in financial planning

These are the most common credentials in the financial planning profession. To earn these designations, these pros have passed a **licensing exam**, or series of tests, in their specialty. They must also complete continuing education to keep their license.

Title	Area(s) of Expertise
Certified Financial Planner (CFP)	A wide range of financial areas, including taxes, investments, and insurance.
Certified Public Accountant (CPA)	Taxes and accounting.
Certified Financial Analyst (CFA)	In-depth knowledge of investments.
Chartered Life Underwriter (CLU)	Life insurance.
Chartered Financial Consultant (ChFC)	Strong focus on insurance, as well as expertise in finance and investing.
Personal Financial Specialist (PFS)	Taxes, accounting, and a wide range of financial areas. PFSs are CPAs who receive additional training in personal finance.

finding a financial planner

Don't be afraid to ask questions

So, you've decided a financial planner is the way to go. You'll want an adviser you are comfortable with and who is also trustworthy, experienced, and intelligent. After all, your planner will be privy to all of your financial information and entrusted with helping you choose an investment strategy. So how do you find the right adviser? Begin by asking the following questions:

- How long have you been in practice and what types of clients do you serve? (Look for someone with clients whose income level, risk tolerance, and investment goals are like yours.)

- How often will you monitor the progress toward my goals? As needed? Every month? Every six months? Once a year? (Find out how much written advice you'll get and how many face-to-face meetings.)

- How do you charge? How much do you charge? Do you sell financial products? How are you connected with the firms whose products you sell? (See page 24 for more on fee-versus commission-based planners.)

- What's your area of expertise? What licenses do you hold? How do you stay current in the field?

- What professional organizations do you belong to? (Ask for the phone numbers of relevant organizations and contact them to see if the planner is a member in good standing. If you are dealing with a CFP, check **www.cfp-board.org**.)

- Do you have any clients I can talk to about their experiences working with you? (Ask the clients: Did the planner do what he said he would? How quickly did he return your phone calls? Are you still using the planner's services? Why or why not?)

- How accessible are you? (Does the planner explain financial strategies clearly? Or does he use a lot of jargon about annualized returns and expect you to follow along? Try to find a planner who speaks a language you understand—and listens well.)

Where to look

The best way to find any professional is through a personal reference. Ask your lawyer, your accountant, and your friends and relatives for the names of financial planners whose services they have used or would recommend. If that doesn't turn up any candidates, your best bet is to contact the following organizations for a recommendation:

- **The Garrett Planning Network** is a national group of financial advisers committed to providing independent, objective financial advice to average consumers. All of their advisers work on an hourly, as-needed, or fee-only basis. Contact them at 1 (877) 510-1500 or visit **www.garrettplanningnetwork.com**.

- **The National Association of Personal Financial Advisors** is a national organization with strict membership requirements for admittance. They provide referrals for fee-only planners; call 1 (888) FEE-ONLY or visit their Web site at **www.napfa.org**.

- **The Financial Planning Association** is a national group of planners. The association's Consumer Service and Planner Search provides information about choosing planners and lets you select planners by zip code. Call 1 (800) 282-PLAN or visit **www.fpanet.org/plannersearch/plannersearch.cfm**.

FIRST-PERSON SUCCESS STORY

Canapés and CFPs

I've always been reserved about money. I don't like to talk about how much I spend and how much I save, especially not with strangers. So whenever my husband and I sat down to figure out our finances—first the amount we'd need for a home, then various expenses that cropped up with the kids like braces and summer camp, and, finally, how to fund a nest egg for retirement and college tuition—we just muddled through. I'm convinced that we didn't have a third child because we thought we couldn't afford it. It wasn't until we had been married for a number of years that a friend told us—at a party, of all places—that she had just hired a financial planner and was finally getting her finances in order. At first, I couldn't believe she was talking about her finances so casually over canapés and cocktails. But the more I listened, the more I liked what I heard. And the more relaxed I felt. That evening, my husband and I both agreed to get some professional help with our finances. Ten years later, we have finally saved up the down payment on a retirement home. I'm sure that if we hadn't sought professional help, we would have never reached this goal.

—Marcia R., Boca Raton, FL

now what do I do?

Answers to common questions

We are finally putting a budget together. My wife thinks that giving our seven-year-old daughter an allowance will help her control the "gimmees" and help us stay on track. Is this a good idea?

Children as young as five can usually manage a small allowance. Since you and your wife are trying to control your spending, an allowance will teach your daughter budgeting skills on a smaller scale and help her feel involved (a necessary component to a successful budget). It will also help you explain, after you put your budget into action, why you must postpone certain purchases. The toughest part of doling out an allowance: figuring out how much to give. Generally, it depends on how much you can afford, what you expect your child to buy with the money, your child's age, and, to some extent, the going rate among other youngsters in your neighborhood. Whatever amount you give, try to adhere to these simple rules:

- Give the money consistently, and on time. (Don't make your child ask for her allowance.)

- Explain to your child what she is expected to buy with the money. Are any purchases, such as junk food, off limits? Once you've established these guidelines, let the child alone. An allowance is, after all, money that she is allowed to spend.

- Don't tie the allowance to chores or grades. Why not? An allowance is meant to teach kids how to budget and to be smart shoppers. It's not a reward for a good report card or payment for tidying their rooms. (If kids want to earn extra money, pay them to do unassigned chores like raking leaves or cleaning out the garage.)

- Don't chip in extra money if your child runs out of cash before the next allowance day.

I recently got married. Should my husband and I pay our bills from a joint checking account?

That's one way to do it. What's the advantage? Since only one account needs to be maintained, it's often easier to keep tabs on your spending. However, some couples—especially dual income ones—find this system limited. They often set up a three-account system instead. A joint account covers joint purchases and expenses like the mortgage and heating bills. Each partner contributes a certain amount each month to this account, depending on how much he or she earns. (A 50/50 split only works if both spouses earn roughly the same amount.) Each spouse also maintains a separate personal account used to buy personal items, such as clothes and gifts. Many couples like this arrangement because it forces them to work together yet still gives them some freedom to make their own purchases without consulting each other. Which system is better? Neither. It depends on your personal situation and preferences.

Now where do I go?

Books

How to Stop Fighting About Money and Make Some
by Adriane G. Berg

Money Doesn't Grow on Trees: A Parent's Guide to Raising Financially Responsible Children
by Neale S. Godfrey and Carolina Edwards

Personal Finance for Dummies
by Eric Tyson

The Smart Woman's Guide to Spending, Saving, and Managing Money
by Diane Pearl and Ellie Williams Clinton

Web Sites

www.simpleliving.com
Articles and tips on how to streamline your life and live more fully without wasting precious time and money trying to "keep up with the Joneses."

www.frugaliving.com
A Web site featuring creative ways to save money and tips for living a satisfying and simple life while building a sustainable community in your neighborhood.

How Much Comes In?

CHAPTER 2

"We got our cash flow under control."

understanding cash flow

Money comes in, money goes out

How much money do you earn each year? How much do you spend? Answering these two questions—and calculating the relationship between what you earn and what you spend—is the next step in the budgeting process. Financial experts call this essential element a **cash flow analysis**. Fortunately, it's not as difficult as it sounds. All you have to do is subtract your monthly or annual expenses from your monthly or annual income. Why is that so important? Your cash flow tells you if you're living within—or above—your means. It can also help you identify your problem spending areas, and show you how much money you have available to save.

If it turns out you earn more than you spend, congratulations. You have what's called a **positive cash flow**. While you won't have to make any major changes to pay your bills and stay out of debt, you'll probably want to—if you hope to reach your financial goals.

If your expenses exceed your income, however, you have a **negative cash flow**. That means you're consistently spending more than you earn, and that's a problem. You can't continue living beyond your means indefinitely. To remedy the situation, you'll have to cut your expenses, boost your income, or both. But . . . we're getting ahead of ourselves. Before you can analyze your cash flow and make any needed adjustments, you must first figure out how much money you earn and how much money you spend. In this chapter, you will learn how to calculate your annual income.

Here's what you'll need to get started:

- Your most recent federal and state income tax returns

- The most recent pay stubs for you and other family members

Lessons from literature

" . . . If a man had 20 pounds a year for his income and spent 19 pounds 19 shillings and 6 pence, he would be happy, but . . . if he spent 20 pounds one he would be miserable."

– Charles Dickens

When Dickens was a child, his father was sent to debtors' prison. There, he gave his son this timeless financial advice. The grown-up Dickens would repeat this advice in the words of his debt-laden character, Mr. Micawber, in his semiautobiographical novel *David Copperfield*. Its simple yet profound meaning? Spend less than you earn.

your paycheck

Your pay stub shows where some of your income goes

The first place to start when figuring out how much money is coming in is your paycheck. Had a good look at your pay stub lately? A sizable chunk of your income is gone before you even cash your paycheck. It can be a shock to see how much your employer and the government take out of your salary. First, your employer probably takes money out of your **gross** (pretax) **salary** to pay for company benefits, such as health and dental insurance, plus retirement plans you have chosen to contribute to, such as your 401(k). Then the federal, state, and sometimes even local governments take money out of your paycheck for taxes and various programs you must contribute to, such as Social Security and Medicare. As a result, the amount you actually get is called your **net** or **take-home salary** (the dollar amount on your check). Pretax deductions such as medical insurance and 401(k) contributions reduce the amount of salary you're required to pay income taxes on. After-tax deductions, however, come right out of your pocket, so there's no tax benefit there.

Employee Name Jane Taxpayer				Social Security No. 010-01-0101

A Earnings	Current Hours	Current Earnings	YTD Hours	YTD Earnings
Regular Earnings	40.00	811.54	1,520.00	30,330.80

ACME INDUSTRIES

Total:	40.00	811.54	1,520.00	30,330.80

Taxes		Current Taxes	YTD Taxes	YTD Taxable
F Fed Withholding		52.50	3,596.05	29,468.00
G Fed FICA Medicare Hospital Ins	11.16	434.35	29,954.90
Fed FICA OASDI		47.69	1,857.20	29,954.00
H New Jersey Withholding		65.34	1,279.14	29,468.00
Total:		176.69	7,166.74	

What your pay stub tells you

A Regular Earnings: Your weekly or biweekly salary or wages. Also called your gross salary.

B Company Medical: What you contribute to have health insurance coverage under your company's medical plan.

C Company Dental: What you contribute to have dental insurance under your company's dental plan.

D Long-term Disability: The amount you pay for coverage under your company's disability insurance program.

E 401(k) Savings Plan: The amount of money you have deducted from your gross salary to be invested in your company's 401(k) retirement program.

F Federal Withholding: The amount of federal taxes taken out by your employer and sent to the IRS on your behalf. The amount is based on how many deductions you claimed on your W-4 form.

G Federal FICA: The amount that is deducted for federal programs such as Social Security, Medicare, and unemployment benefits.

H State Withholding: Money that is withheld to pay for your state taxes.

Period Beginning 9/08/03	Period Ending 9/14/03	Rate $811.54	
Deductions	Before Tax Deductions	After Tax Deductions	YTD Deductions
Medical— B	8.95		377.90
C —Dental	1.00		38.00
Long-term Disability— D		.45	18.77
E —401(k)	40.57		486.90
Total:	50.52	.45	921.57
		Current Taxable Benefits	YTD Taxable Benefits

regular income

**Payments you
can count on**

Salary from a job is the largest source of income for most folks. But income also includes two other kinds of payments: regular income (other payments of a fixed amount you receive every week, month, or year), and irregular income, which are payments of varying amounts that you may or may not receive more than once.

Below, you'll find the various types of regular income that most people encounter.

■ **Salaried income** This is the largest source of regular income for most people. Salaried income does not include tips and bonuses, which are irregular payments.

■ **Support payments** Alimony and child support are usually considered regular income. If you're laid off or out of work due to a disability, you may receive support payments in the form of unemployment benefits, workers' compensation payments, or disability income replacement, which comes through your disability insurance.

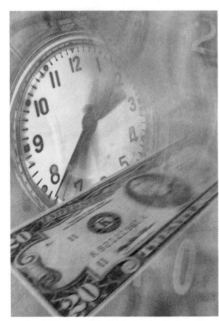

■ **Investment income** This may be the most complicated category simply because there are so many options. Your savings accounts pay interest regularly, as do your money market accounts (both the bank and the mutual fund variety) and your certificates of deposit. Stocks, bonds, mutual funds, and Treasury securities also may pay dividends.

■ **Retirement income** Once you retire, you'll probably start receiving monthly Social Security payments and/or a monthly pension. You'll also begin withdrawing money from the retirement accounts you have funded throughout your working life, such as your 401(k), IRA, or Keogh plans. (Once you reach the age of 70½, you must withdraw a minimum amount each year.) If your spouse has also retired, include those payments, too.

ASK THE  EXPERTS

I know how much I'll earn from my job this year, but I don't know how much interest and dividends I'll earn from my investments. Any suggestions?

For a ballpark estimate, use last year's tax return numbers. In most cases, you hopefully will be underestimating (and not overestimating) your income. Why? Ideally, your interest earnings should increase from one year to the next because a) your savings will have grown and will thus generate more interest; b) the companies whose stocks you own will have grown too and, thus, may generate larger dividend payments; and c) you may have socked away more money this year which, again, should be generating larger interest payments.

My 16-year-old son works part time at the local grocery store. Should I include his wages in the family income?

Probably not. His salary is most likely going toward his own expenses, such as clothing or entertainment. You can teach him more about managing money—and ease your own financial burden—by clearly outlining what he's expected to do with his salary. Is he expected to buy his own lunch, for example? How about buying school supplies and clothes or contributing to a college fund? Then, erase those expenses from your own budget.

FIRST-PERSON SUCCESS STORY

Late bloomer

Negative cash flow? Positive cash flow? It's all Greek to me. As long as I can pay my bills, I must be doing okay, right? That's the way I handled my finances for—I hate to admit it—almost 10 years. But when I turned 35 and decided to buy a home, one look at my bank book told me that I needed to start saving in a serious way. The next day, I began tracking what I earned—and spent. I was shocked to find out how much money was literally slipping through my fingers. Over the next five years, I kept close tabs on my cash flow. When I finally bought my first home two weeks ago, it was truly a dream come true. But standing on the front porch and watching the leaves change colors on the big oak tree in my front yard, I can't help but think: If I had had a financial plan in place from the start, I would have been enjoying this home sweet home years ago.

—Susannah R., Lexington, KY

irregular income

Keeping tabs on those surprise payments

Irregular income consists of payments that you do not receive on a consistent basis, or payments that you receive regularly, but that vary in amount. Some sources of irregular income include:

- **Bonuses and tips** This category includes sales commissions, performances bonuses, and/or tips.

- **Self-employment income** If you work for yourself and your salary depends on your profits each month, your earnings belong in this category. Royalties received from the sale of a book you've written—or as a result of some other creative endeavor—should go here, too.

- **Other income** What goes here? Inheritance money, trust fund payments, lottery winnings, and the rental income from your vacation home! Seriously, here's the place to note any remaining sources of income that just don't fit elsewhere.

ASK THE EXPERTS

I'm a waitress and my tips vary from week to week and from season to season. How do I estimate them when creating a budget?

One thing you can try is recording your daily tips for three months, then dividing the total by the number of days you worked to give you a daily average. Though this probably won't be an exact number, it's good enough. Ideally, you should track your income and expenses for three months anyway to see where your money is going before creating a budget.

I work on a freelance basis, so I don't get a regular paycheck. How do I estimate my future income if I don't know how much I'm going to earn each month?

Good question. Since your income fluctuates from month to month, you need to do some forecasting. Look at how much money you earned last year. Is it reasonable to expect that you'll earn a similar amount this year? Use that figure as your projected income amount. Perhaps the business you work in, however, is booming and you expect to be offered more assignments. Based on that assessment, you may want to project a higher income for next year. What if you guess wrong and your work doesn't increase as planned? You can always adjust the income figures later on, if necessary. Revision is a normal part of the budgeting process.

I am supposed to receive a $20,000 inheritance at the end of this year or beginning of next. How do I include this in my income calculations if I don't know when I'll get it?

Unless you plan to spend it all as soon as you get it, exclude it from your income calculations. Instead, plan to use the money for significant items. For example, set it aside for retirement, use it to pay off credit card debt, or put it toward your child's education.

income worksheet

How much money does your family earn each year?

On the preceding pages, you've looked at the various types of income. Now it's time to put some dollar figures next to those items. This worksheet should help you get started. Where applicable, simply fill in the appropriate spaces. Don't have a particular type of income? Simply leave that line blank. It is the rare person who has all these types of income.

	MONTHLY AMOUNT	YEARLY AMOUNT
1. Salaried Income		
Your net take-home pay	_____	_____
Bonuses	_____	_____
Commissions	_____	_____
Tips	_____	_____
Overtime pay	_____	_____
Second job	_____	_____
Spouse's take-home pay	_____	_____
Spouse's bonuses	_____	_____
Spouse's commissions	_____	_____
Spouse's tips	_____	_____
Spouse's overtime pay	_____	_____
Spouse's second job	_____	_____
Total Salaried Income	_____	_____
2. Self-Employment Income		
Self-employment income	_____	_____
Royalties	_____	_____
Freelance income	_____	_____
Business/partnership income	_____	_____
Other	_____	_____
Total Self-Employment Income	_____	_____

	MONTHLY AMOUNT	YEARLY AMOUNT

3. Additional Income

	MONTHLY AMOUNT	YEARLY AMOUNT
Alimony payments	_____	_____
Child support payments	_____	_____
Disability payments	_____	_____
Unemployment benefits	_____	_____
Workers' compensation payments	_____	_____
Other	_____	_____
Total Additional Income	_____	_____

4. Investment Income
(Note: Most experts recommend reinvesting any investment income you earn until you retire, at which point this income might be used to supplement your retirement income. Therefore, you may want to think twice before including investment income in your total income.)

Interest Payments

	MONTHLY AMOUNT	YEARLY AMOUNT
Savings account	_____	_____
Money-market account	_____	_____
Certificates of deposit	_____	_____
Bonds	_____	_____
Other	_____	_____

Dividends

	MONTHLY AMOUNT	YEARLY AMOUNT
Stocks	_____	_____
Mutual funds	_____	_____
Other	_____	_____
Total Investment Income	_____	_____

income worksheet cont'd

	MONTHLY AMOUNT	YEARLY AMOUNT
5. Retirement Income		
Social security payments	_____	_____
Yours	_____	_____
Spouse's	_____	_____
IRA payments	_____	_____
Yours	_____	_____
Spouse's	_____	_____
401(k) or similar plan payments	_____	_____
Yours	_____	_____
Spouse's	_____	_____
Pension/annuity payments	_____	_____
Yours	_____	_____
Spouse's	_____	_____
Keogh/profit-sharing payments	_____	_____
Yours	_____	_____
Spouse's	_____	_____
Total Retirement Income	_____	_____
6. Other Income		
Inheritance (see page 39)	_____	_____
Cash gifts	_____	_____
Lottery winnings?!	_____	_____
Rental income	_____	_____
Other	_____	_____
Total Other Income	_____	_____

What's your total?

It's time to add everything up. Simply fill in the blanks below with the various total amounts from each section of the worksheet.

	MONTHLY AMOUNT	YEARLY AMOUNT
1. Total Salaried Income	_____	_____
2. Total Self-Employment Income	_____	_____
3. Total Additional Income	_____	_____
4. Total Investment Income	_____	_____
5. Total Retirement Income	_____	_____
6. Total Other Income	_____	_____
TOTAL INCOME	_____	_____

The Bottom Line

You may be surprised by how much—or how little—your total income actually is. You may even be a little disappointed. Four pages worth of charts and what do you have to show for it? A simple tally of how much you and your spouse bring in. The figure doesn't tell you how much of that money you spend, or how much of that money you save. But a total income figure is an integral part of every budget. In the next chapter, we will add up all of the money you spend. That amount will then be subtracted from your total income to give you your cash flow.

now what do I do?

Answers to common questions

What's the difference between my gross salary and my net salary? Which one should I use when budgeting?

Your gross salary is the total amount that you earn before taxes, health insurance premiums, and other items are deducted from your salary. Your net salary, on the other hand, is the amount you "net," or take home, after those deductions are withdrawn. If you're a regular, salaried worker (that is, you don't work for yourself or own a business), it's best—and easiest—for budgeting purposes to use your net salary. Why? That's the amount of money you actually get: your paycheck. (See page 34.)

What if I'm self-employed? Do I use my net or gross salary?

You can use either. It depends on how complicated your situation is and how precise you want to be. If you have lots of business expenses, you may prefer using the net salary—your gross salary minus your business expenses—the ones you stated on your tax return. Otherwise, you will have to itemize all your expenses on your household or a separate expense worksheet. If you have just a handful of expenses, on the other hand, you could simply use your gross salary and include your business expenses along with your household expenses. Either way it's essential to remember that taxes are not automatically withdrawn from your paycheck as they are with a salaried job. Generally, you have to pay estimated income and self-employment taxes on a quarterly basis. These figures should be listed as expenses in the worksheets in the next chapter.

I'm expecting a raise in four months. Should I figure the raise into my budgeted income?

You should only include it if the increase is a significant amount or will significantly affect your financial picture. And wait until you get the raise to see how it factors into your actual cash flow. For example, although you may get a 3% annual raise on your salary, you may not see a 3% increase in the amount of your monthly disposable income. Why? If this is a typical cost-of-living raise, intended to help your income keep pace with inflation, you can expect a similar rise in your expenses over the year. So you really should only count that raise if it is significantly more than the typical 3% annual inflation rate and if it really does add up to more disposable income every month. Too complicated? Another option is just to ignore the raise and sock it away in a savings plan, then later use the additional income to pay down debt or boost savings.

Do I have to pay taxes on the unemployment benefits I receive? That hardly seems fair since I no longer have a job.

Uncle Sam has generously arranged for you to receive payments while you're unemployed. Unfortunately, he's not that generous. You must pay federal income tax on this money—just as you would with your ordinary income. So be sure to set aside at least 20% of your unemployment benefits for taxes.

What is the difference between "take-home pay" and "disposable income"?

Take-home pay is the money you have left from your salary after taxes are withdrawn. Disposable income, on the other hand, refers to the money you have left from your salary after taxes are withdrawn—and which you use to pay your everyday expenses. Disposable income typically does not include income earned from stock dividends, interest from a savings account, or other investment income, since you typically reinvest this kind of income right away to build more wealth for yourself before retiring.

Now where do I go?

Books

The Wealthy Barber: Everyone's Commonsense Guide to Becoming Financially Independent
by David B. Chilton
A handy guide to personal finance, with a twist: It's written in novel form!

How to Get What You Want in Life with the Money You Already Have
by Carol Keeffe
Offers simple yet revolutionary solutions for realizing your financial dreams.

Ninety Days to Financial Fitness
by Joan German-Grapes
Offers model financial plans for married couples, singles, and people in other situations.

Your Money or Your Life: Transforming Your Relationship with Money and Achieving Financial Independence
by Joe R. Dominguez and Vicki Robin
A revolutionary and empowering nine-step program for building financial security.

Web Sites

www.quicken.com
Tips on investing and managing your money, as well as an online money management program.

www.smartmoney.com
Great general consumer finance Web site.

How Much Goes Out?

Chapter 3

"I never knew where all the money was going before."

spending habits

Find out where your money goes

Where does your money go? Like many people, you probably don't know—not exactly anyway. There's your mortgage, the car payment, heat and electric bills, clothes, and, of course, food. Most of us can figure that much out. But what happens to the rest of your paycheck? How much money do you spend each month? What do you spend it on?

To find out, you will need the records of your daily expenses, which you have been jotting down in your spending diary (see page 12). You need to account for everything: not just last night's restaurant tab, but also the $15 worth of gas that you just pumped and that pint of ice cream you picked up on the way home from the office. Isn't this a bit nit picky? You bet. Nobody ever said tracking expenses was fun or exciting. But it can make a world of difference to your finances.

In addition figuring out what you spend your money on, you also need to find out how you are spending it. Do you use your paycheck to cover most of your expenses? Do you rack up impulse purchases on your credit card, promising yourself that you will pay them off right away (and not doing so)?

As you start noting the methods you use to cover your expenses, patterns will start to reveal themselves. For example, you may notice that toward the end of each month, there are increased clothing expenses. Did you realize you were splurging each month on this?

And when it comes to budgeting, just knowing how you're spending your money is half the battle. You will be able to create a budget that can help you meet your financial goals at last, whatever they may be.

Five good reasons to track your spending

1. You'll find out where you spent all the cash you withdrew from ATMs.

2. You'll find out where you spent all the money you owe on your credit cards.

3. You'll find your "cash leaks." Once you identify this wasteful spending, you can plug the holes.

4. You'll find out how much you're saving—or not.

5. You'll find out if you're spending more money on luxury items than on your necessities.

So why is all this important? Because knowledge is power. By finding out where your money is going, you are arming yourself with the knowledge you need to make smarter financial decisions in the future.

Your plan of action

Tracking daily expenses in a spending notebook for three months is vital. If you have not already begun to do this (see page 12), you should now.

Start with daily expenses like carfare and lunch. Be sure to include even small purchases such as a newspaper or a cup of coffee. Eventually you will transfer this information to the Expense worksheet found on pages 54–63.

1. Salaried Income	MONTHLY AMOUNT	YEARLY AMOUNT
Your net take-home pay	$2,500.00	
Bonuses		$30,000.00
Commissions		$500.00
Tips		
Overtime pay	$200.00	
Second job		$2,400.00
Spouse's take-home pay	$3,000.00	
Spouse's bonuses		$36,000.00
Spouse's commissions		
Spouse's tips	$100.00	
Spouse's overtime pay		$1,200.00
Spouse's second job		
Total Salaried Income	$5,800.00	$70,100.00

types of expenses

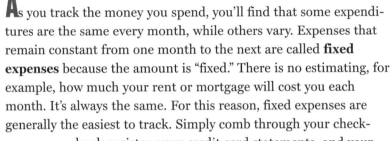

Some expenses stay the same, others don't

As you track the money you spend, you'll find that some expenditures are the same every month, while others vary. Expenses that remain constant from one month to the next are called **fixed expenses** because the amount is "fixed." There is no estimating, for example, how much your rent or mortgage will cost you each month. It's always the same. For this reason, fixed expenses are generally the easiest to track. Simply comb through your checkbook register, your credit card statements, and your savings and investment account statements to find the numbers. To make sure that you don't count any payments more than once, circle or check off each item as you transfer the amount to your expense worksheet.

Most fixed expenses—such as rent or car payments—represent basic necessities. However, if your goal is to reduce your spending, there may be some fixed expenses you can live without. For example, you may pay a fixed amount of $49.95 per month for cable TV, but do you really need cable?

Expenses that you pay regularly—but that vary in the amount you pay each month—are called **variable expenses**. Variable expenses are less predictable than fixed expenses. For example, one month your electric bill might be $40, another month it might be $100. In the case of some variable expenses, such as food and clothing, this flexibility gives you more control over how much you spend and when; however, it also makes it harder to gauge how much you actually spend each month.

Finally, there's a third type of expense, called a **discretionary expense**, which is, perhaps, the toughest to track. Why? Because these purchases don't occur every month and are generally for nonessential items—think gifts, movie tickets, and the like. People often "forget" that they actually spend this money. This is the cash that falls through those proverbial cracks. When you have to reduce your spending, though, this is often the easiest category to cut back on.

ASK THE EXPERTS

I rarely eat out and don't seem to have many discretionary expenses. How will I be able to cut my spending?

In the worksheets that follow, you'll use your daily spending diary to fill in monthly tallies for expenses that range from the common (groceries and heat) to the truly luxurious (massages and facials). If the categories do not apply to your life, take a pen and add or delete items as needed. Once you start tracking your spending, you may find that you're actually spending more than you think on, say, movie rentals. More than you want to, in fact. That's the point of this exercise: to find hidden "black holes" into which your money disappears. Most people have a few, and once you find yours, you can create a budget (see Chapter 6) and start cutting back on your discretionary, or "luxury" expenses.

If it turns out, however, that you are one of the rare people who does not have any spending "black holes," but whose income just covers your fixed and variable expenses, leaving little money to throw around, then you might want to think of ways in which you can cut back on some of your fixed and variable expenses. For example, you might consider renting a less expensive apartment or taking in a boarder or housemate. You could also try switching to a cheaper cell phone plan, turning down your thermostat to cut back on heating bills, bringing your lunch to work, or cooking rather than dining out.

hidden costs

Once you get the hang of tracking expenses, monthly bills are relatively easy to monitor. Unfortunately, all expenses don't fit into neat, monthly categories. Lawn care bills are high in spring and summer months, nonexistent in cold weather. Likewise, you usually get hit with hefty bills for heat in winter only. And your car insurance and life insurance payments are typically paid once per year. Because you don't pay these bills monthly, it can be easy to overlook them when figuring your expenses.

Even if you do remember to plan ahead for expenses like these, they can be easy to underbudget, and this is one of the main reasons why many budgets fail. Take home renovations, for example: They often end up costing more than expected. And vacations: Many people set aside funds for the trip itself—airfare, hotel, and meals. Often, though, they forget costly incidentals that are part of every trip: souvenirs and T-shirts, admission fees at museums and amusement parks, and the never-ending flow of soft drinks and ice cream cones. Unless you set money aside for these periodic and unanticipated expenses—or have a cash reserve fund to draw on—you may be forced to put these bills on a credit card.

Finally, there are the unanticipated or unplanned-for expenses, which are even harder to budget for. The car breaks down. Your son needs another gift for yet another birthday party. Your brother needs a loan. When figuring your expenses, you can create a separate "slush fund" category for such surprise expenses and assign a reasonable estimate, or you can make a guess based on the total you shell out for unexpected expenses during your three-month recordkeeping period.

So . . . how do you deal with all these unanticipated expenses? Make a list of every foreseeable expense within the next year. That means include the cost of your bridemaid's outfit for a friend's wedding—and matching shoes and fancy updo—even if it's only August and the wedding is not until next May. Assign an annual cost to each expense. Then divide by 12 to come up with a monthly amount, and itemize those expenses on the worksheet on page 62.

Typical unanticipated costs

- car repairs
- appliance repairs
- home decorating
- holiday decorating
- gifts (not just holiday gifts, but gifts for birthdays, anniversaries, graduations, Mother's Day, baby showers, etc.)
- medical and dental bills
- eyeglasses
- school trips; school fundraisers; school supplies
- dance recital costumes
- music lessons
- sports equipment; team fees; camps or clinics
- flowers; shrubs; mulch
- snow removal
- carpet cleaning
- tax preparation fees

FIRST-PERSON DISASTER STORY

Speed bump

I'm not sure how it all happened. I had just graduated from college and was out on my own, working at my first job. Naturally, my salary barely covered my expenses. And then there was the student loan to pay off. Still, I had some extra cash to play with—so I spent every cent of it. Dinner with friends. Concert tickets. A new work wardrobe. Then, reality hit. My annual car insurance bill arrived in my mailbox. I had completely forgotten about it. How was I going to come up with $1,500? I had $25 to my name—and that had to last me until the next payday. Ultimately, I had to ask my parents for a loan. Now I'm paying back a small amount each month. And I'm also depositing a similar amount in my checking account each month to cover future expenses that I just might happen to "forget" about.

—Ella J., DePere, WI

fixed expenses worksheet

Items for which you pay a monthly "fixed" amount

This worksheet is a no-brainer. Really. Since these are all fixed expenses, there's no estimating or tracking involved. If you have a mortgage, for example, simply review your coupon payment book or your check register to see how much you pay to the bank each month. It's that simple.

EXPENSE	MONTHLY AMOUNT
1. Housing	_____
Rent	_____
Mortgage condo/co-op fees	_____
Property taxes	_____
Total Fixed Housing Expenses	_____
2. Insurance	_____
Homeowner's/renter's	_____
Auto	_____
Dental	_____
Health	_____
Disability	_____
Life	_____
Long-term care	_____
Other	_____
Total Fixed Insurance Expenses	_____
3. Transportation	_____
Auto loan payment	_____
Auto lease payment	_____
Commuting (bus, train, taxi)	_____
Parking	_____
Tolls	_____
Total Fixed Transportation Expenses	_____

EXPENSE	MONTHLY AMOUNT
4. Family	_____
Child support payments	_____
Alimony payments	_____
Tuition	_____
Child care, baby-sitting	_____
Total Fixed Family Expenses	_____
5. Utilities	_____
Electricity/water/sewage	_____
Trash and/or recycling service	_____
Telephone (basic service)	_____
Heat	_____
Cable TV	_____
Computer online services	_____
Cell phone service	_____
Other	_____
Total Fixed Utilities Expenses	_____
6. Debt	_____
School loan payments	_____
Home equity loan payments, second mortgage	_____
Minimum credit card payments	_____
Other	_____
Total Fixed Debt Expenses	_____
7. Special savings accounts	_____
401(k)	_____
IRA	_____
College fund	_____
Mutual fund	_____
Money market account	_____
Other	_____
Total Fixed Savings Expenses	_____
TOTAL FIXED EXPENSES (Add lines 1 through 7)	_____

variable expenses worksheet

**These expenses
vary from month
to month**

Yes, it'll take some time and effort to fill out this detailed list of
expenses. But when you're done, you will know exactly where your
money goes—and you'll be able to use this vital knowledge to draw
up a successful spending plan.

To fill in the blanks below, you'll have to review your checkbook,
credit card statements, and that little notebook you've been using
to track your expenses for three months. (Don't worry about the
"average" column yet. We'll explain that at the end of the worksheet.) Feel free to delete and/or add expenses to reflect your
lifestyle. The items listed under each heading are meant to guide—
not limit—you.

As you go along, think about which expenses you might be able to
cut out or reduce when the time comes to create your budget.

EXPENSE	MONTH #1	MONTH #2	MONTH #3	AVERAGE
1. Housing				
repairs	_____	_____	_____	_____
renovations	_____	_____	_____	_____
furniture	_____	_____	_____	_____
appliances	_____	_____	_____	_____
decorating	_____	_____	_____	_____
linens/bedding/curtains	_____	_____	_____	_____
cleaning service	_____	_____	_____	_____
security system	_____	_____	_____	_____
lawn/garden	_____	_____	_____	_____
pool maintenance	_____	_____	_____	_____
curtain/rug cleaning	_____	_____	_____	_____
pest control	_____	_____	_____	_____
Total Housing	_____	_____	_____	_____

EXPENSE	MONTH #1	MONTH #2	MONTH #3	AVERAGE
2. Transportation				
gas	_____	_____	_____	_____
maintenance	_____	_____	_____	_____
tolls	_____	_____	_____	_____
parking	_____	_____	_____	_____
mass transit fares	_____	_____	_____	_____
repairs	_____	_____	_____	_____
car wash	_____	_____	_____	_____
Total Transportation	_____	_____	_____	_____
3. Utilities				
long-distance phone charges	_____	_____	_____	_____
electricity	_____	_____	_____	_____
gas	_____	_____	_____	_____
Total Utilities	_____	_____	_____	_____
4. Food				
groceries	_____	_____	_____	_____
take-out or restaurant meals	_____	_____	_____	_____
morning coffee	_____	_____	_____	_____
candy/gum/snacks	_____	_____	_____	_____
wine/liquor	_____	_____	_____	_____
at-home parties	_____	_____	_____	_____
vitamins or supplements	_____	_____	_____	_____
Total Food	_____	_____	_____	_____

variable expenses worksheet cont'd

EXPENSE	MONTH #1	MONTH #2	MONTH #3	AVERAGE
5. Clothing				
work clothes	_____	_____	_____	_____
casual clothes	_____	_____	_____	_____
sports clothes	_____	_____	_____	_____
school clothes	_____	_____	_____	_____
footwear	_____	_____	_____	_____
outerwear	_____	_____	_____	_____
accessories/jewelry	_____	_____	_____	_____
sleepwear	_____	_____	_____	_____
underwear/socks	_____	_____	_____	_____
tailoring	_____	_____	_____	_____
dry cleaning	_____	_____	_____	_____
Total Clothing	_____	_____	_____	_____
6. Medical and Dental				
eyeglasses/contact lenses	_____	_____	_____	_____
eye exams	_____	_____	_____	_____
prescriptions	_____	_____	_____	_____
over-the-counter medicines	_____	_____	_____	_____
copayments	_____	_____	_____	_____
nonreimbursed expenses	_____	_____	_____	_____
dental bills	_____	_____	_____	_____
orthodontia bills	_____	_____	_____	_____
other	_____	_____	_____	_____
Total Medical and Dental	_____	_____	_____	_____

EXPENSE	MONTH #1	MONTH #2	MONTH #3	AVERAGE
7. Children				
diapers	_____	_____	_____	_____
formula	_____	_____	_____	_____
day camp or summer camp	_____	_____	_____	_____
birthday parties	_____	_____	_____	_____
class trips	_____	_____	_____	_____
day care	_____	_____	_____	_____
babysitter	_____	_____	_____	_____
music/dance lessons	_____	_____	_____	_____
music/dance equipment	_____	_____	_____	_____
sports teams or lessons	_____	_____	_____	_____
sporting equipment	_____	_____	_____	_____
computer	_____	_____	_____	_____
computer/video games	_____	_____	_____	_____
prom	_____	_____	_____	_____
yearbook/class ring	_____	_____	_____	_____
toys/games	_____	_____	_____	_____
allowances	_____	_____	_____	_____
Total Children	_____	_____	_____	_____

variable expenses worksheet cont'd

EXPENSE	MONTH #1	MONTH #2	MONTH #3	AVERAGE
8. Recreation				
theater/concert tickets				
movie tickets				
video rentals				
sporting events/equipment				
books				
magazine/newspaper subscriptions				
CDs/DVDs/videos				
vacations				
airline/train tickets				
hobbies				
gym membership/dues				
club membership/dues				
computer software				
gambling/lottery tickets				
Total Recreation				
9. Personal Care				
haircut				
highlights/color/perm				
manicure/pedicure				
body care (massage, etc.)				
cosmetics				
hair care products				
personal hygiene products				
Total Personal Care				

EXPENSE	MONTH #1	MONTH #2	MONTH #3	AVERAGE
10. Pets				
grooming	_____	_____	_____	_____
pet food	_____	_____	_____	_____
vet bills	_____	_____	_____	_____
toys/supplies	_____	_____	_____	_____
kennel boarding	_____	_____	_____	_____
walking service	_____	_____	_____	_____
Total Pets	_____	_____	_____	_____
11. Professional Fees				
lawyer	_____	_____	_____	_____
financial planner	_____	_____	_____	_____
tax preparer	_____	_____	_____	_____
bank fees	_____	_____	_____	_____
annual credit card fees	_____	_____	_____	_____
brokerage commissions	_____	_____	_____	_____
Total Prof'l Fees	_____	_____	_____	_____
12. Taxes and Interest				
reserved for federal taxes	_____	_____	_____	_____
reserved for state taxes	_____	_____	_____	_____
reserved for local taxes	_____	_____	_____	_____
credit card interest	_____	_____	_____	_____
Total Taxes and Interest	_____	_____	_____	_____

variable expenses worksheet cont'd

EXPENSE	MONTH #1	MONTH #2	MONTH #3	AVERAGE
13. Holidays and Gifts	_____	_____	_____	_____
decorations	_____	_____	_____	_____
greeting cards and wrapping paper	_____	_____	_____	_____
holiday activities/events	_____	_____	_____	_____
birthday gifts	_____	_____	_____	_____
holiday gifts	_____	_____	_____	_____
anniversary gifts	_____	_____	_____	_____
wedding/engagement gifts	_____	_____	_____	_____
bridal/baby shower gifts	_____	_____	_____	_____
Total Holidays and Gifts	_____	_____	_____	_____
14. Miscellaneous				
cigarettes	_____	_____	_____	_____
stamps/postage	_____	_____	_____	_____
church/charity contributions	_____	_____	_____	_____
nonsubscription magazines and newspapers	_____	_____	_____	_____
other	_____	_____	_____	_____
unanticipated expenses	_____	_____	_____	_____
Total Miscellaneous	_____	_____	_____	_____

What are your expenses?

It's time to add up your variable expenses. Here's an example. Your worksheet looks like this:

	MONTH #1	MONTH #2	MONTH #3
work clothes	$125.00	$75.00	$100.00

1. Add up the three numbers.
$125
$ 75
+$100=
$300

2. Divide the total amount spent by the number of months.
$300 divided by 3 = $100

3. The answer is the average amount you spent. In this example, it's $100.

4. Your task now? Compute the average of each expense listed. Put the result in the "average" column on the worksheet.

5. Then, simply fill in the blanks below with the total averaged amounts from each section of the Variable Expenses worksheet.

MONTHLY AVERAGE

Housing	_____
Transportation	_____
Utilities	_____
Food	_____
Clothing	_____
Medical and Dental	_____
Children	_____
Recreation	_____
Personal Care	_____
Pets	_____
Professional Fees	_____
Taxes and Interest	_____
Holidays and Gifts	_____
Miscellaneous	_____
TOTAL VARIABLE EXPENSES	_____

your bottom line

And the answer is?!

How do your expenses stack up against your income? That's the answer we have been working toward by having you track your spending for three months and fill in page after page of worksheets. Fortunately, we're almost there. Just a few more quick calculations. (Honest.)

1. Write your total monthly fixed expenses here (from page 55). _____

2. Multiply the amount on line 1 by 12. The result is your annual fixed expenses. Write the amount here. _____

3. Write your total monthly variable expenses here (from page 63). _____

4. Multiply the amount on line 3 by 12. The answer is your annual variable expenses. Write the amount here. _____

5. Add lines 2 and 4 together. The result is your total annual expenses. Write the amount here. _____

6. On this line, write your total annual income figure from page 43 in Chapter 2. _____

7. Subtract the amount on line 5. Write the amount here. _____

The result? Your cash flow. This will be a negative or positive number. If it's not positive, don't panic! Help is on the way!

Taking stock

So . . . how are you doing? There are three basic ways this cash flow information can play out.

- **Your income comfortably exceeds your expenses** Great! You have a positive cash flow. You won't have to make any changes in your spending habits to pay your regular bills and stay out of debt. Should you want to save and invest more money, however, you will need to reduce your expenses.

- **Your income and earnings are about equal** This is not a bad situation to be in. You are certainly living within your means. But you could do with a bit more breathing room, and you probably could be saving more too. To do so, you will need to cut back on your expenses, starting with discretionary items.

- **You spend more than you earn** While this isn't an outcome to cheer about, you're certainly not alone. Study after study shows that Americans spend more than they earn—a lot more. More encouraging news? You can fix the problem by cutting your spending. We'll show you how to do this in the following chapters, so stay tuned.

Pound wise and penny foolish

When you spend more than you earn, your income probably isn't the culprit. The real problem? Your spending. Some families earn $45,000 per year—yet still manage to own a home, go on vacation, and save for retirement. Other families earn $450,000 per year—and can't make ends meet. Go figure.

---

now what do I do?

Answers to common questions

Why do we calculate fixed and variable expenses separately?

Categorizing your expenses this way helps you get a better handle on how much you spend—and how you can cut your costs. Fixed expenses, for example, include living expenses. Generally, you can't cut those too easily. (If your mortgage is too steep for your salary, for example, you must refinance your loan—or sell the house and move to a cheaper home.) Variable expenses, on the other hand, include some living expenses and many discretionary expenses that can be cut easily and quickly. (Need to cut back your clothing tab? Wear last season's winter coat—again.)

I'm spending far less than I earn. Do I really still need to budget?

Budgeting is alway a good idea, even if you always have money left over at the end of the month. Why? Because a budget isn't meant to restrict every impulse to spend. Rather, it's a guide to help you meet your financial goals. A good budget will show you how much money you spend on certain things—and where you can cut costs, if necessary, to save up for that European vacation or a down payment on a house. Even if you don't wish to make any changes in your spending and saving patterns right now, it can still be an eye-opening experience to see how much you earn and how much you spend.

My wife and I can't seem to communicate about our money without arguing. Any advice?

Ruth Hayden wrote a great money guide for couples called *For Richer, Not Poorer*. In it, she describes how to structure regular "money meetings" with your partner in order to discuss how things are going and to help you plan your spending together. During your money meetings, do your best to defuse any emotional issues surrounding money by approaching your joint finances as objectively as possible, looking at them as a financial planner would.

I can't seem to stay motivated to stick to my spending plan. Do you have any suggestions?

Don't give up yet! Your budget is the foundation of your financial plan. Figuring out how much you are spending and what it will take to enable you to maintain that lifestyle in retirement will probably serve as a wake–up call, motivating you even more powerfully to stick to your budget. Another way to get your budget in gear is to promise yourself some kind of reward if you reach a certain goal—just be sure it's something inexpensive, or you'll end up ruining all your hard work! For example, if you reach your goal of cutting $50 off your entertainment budget, you could reward yourself with a lazy Saturday morning in bed, followed by a leisurely, relaxing bath.

How can I follow a monthly budget if I get paid every two weeks (26 times per year)? Some months I get two paychecks; other months I get three.

One way is to budget your expenses to live on just 24 paychecks—that's two paychecks per month for the entire year. There will be two months each year during which you'll receive an "extra" paycheck, but you should just continue on as if you only received two paychecks. Then use that extra paycheck to pay down debt, take a vacation, contribute to a savings plan, establish an emergency fund, or take care of other expenses.

Now where do I go?

Books

Financial Fitness for Life
by Jerry Mason

You've Earned It, Don't Lose It
by Suze Orman

The Richest Man in Babylon
by George Claussen

Master Your Money or It Will Master You
by Arlo Moehlenpah

Web Sites

www.cheapskatemonthly.com
Upbeat site offers tips on cutting spending, conquering debt, and getting your finances under control.

www.greedyfools.com
Comprehensive site offers a range of articles related to saving money and covers the latest financial news.

www.frugaltimes.com
Newsletter with helpful tips on living cheaply and saving with coupons.

Taking Inventory

How much are you worth? 70
Net worth equals your assets minus your liabilities

Understanding your assets 72
Take stock of what you own

Converting assets to cash 74
How easily can you cash in your assets?

Assets worksheet 76
Note everything you own—and what it's worth

Understanding your liabilities 78
Money that you owe

Debt worksheet 80
Do you know how much you owe?

Where do you stand? 82
A negative net worth means too many debts

Now what do I do? 84
Answers to common questions

CHAPTER 4

"Our net worth is better than we realized."

how much are you worth?

Your net worth is a snapshot of your current financial health

Now that you've determined your cash flow, it's time to figure out your **net worth**. What is this? It's what you own, such as your house, car, savings, and stocks (known as **assets**), minus what you owe, such as your mortgage, car loan, student loans, and credit card debt (known as **liabilities**).

What's the point of such a calculation? Think of it as an annual physical exam—except this test measures your fiscal fitness. While your cash flow tells you how much money comes in (your earnings) and how much money goes out (your expenses), your net worth tells you what kind of financial shape you are in overall. And this will help you set realistic budgeting goals. For example, if you have a positive cash flow but a negative net worth (due to car loans and credit card bills), a good budget will help you direct some of that extra income to paying down your debts and building financial security.

Calculating your net worth is important for other reasons, too. You'll need this information when applying for a loan, writing a will, or buying insurance. Lenders, for example, will check your debt-to-income ratio when you apply for a mortgage. And universities ask detailed questions about parents' assets and debts when a teenager applies for college financial aid. Your net worth also serves as a benchmark with which to compare your financial progress. Do you have more credit card debt today than you did 10 years ago? Has your home increased in value? Have you borrowed against your assets? Your goal, naturally, is to raise your net worth over time—which a budget will help you do. But before you can draw up this all-important budget (we'll get to that in Chapter 6), you must first have a clear idea of what you own, how much it's worth, and how much debt you currently owe.

Getting started

Never calculated your net worth before? Not to worry. The explanations and worksheets that follow make it easy. And, if you're computer savvy, you can run these numbers on most personal software programs. To get started, you'll simply need to gather the following items:

1. Your checkbook

2. The most recent statements for your...
   - bank savings account
   - credit union savings account
   - investment accounts (money market, mutual fund, brokerage)
   - IRAs (regular, Roth, and SEP)
   - Keogh plans
   - 401(k) or similar retirement plans
   - college savings account
   - mortgage
   - credit cards
   - car loans
   - student loans
   - home equity loans
   - loans against your insurance policy or 401(k)

3. Any records, receipts, or documents relating to...
   - life insurance policies that have a cash value
   - Certificates of Deposit (CDs)
   - stocks or bonds (not invested through a brokerage account or a mutual fund company)
   - U.S. savings bonds and other treasury securities
   - computers, faxes, and other home office equipment
   - stereos, televisions, and other home entertainment equipment
   - antiques, jewelry, and other valuables

4. A national newspaper like the *Wall Street Journal* or the *New York Times*

5. A copy of your latest income tax return

understanding your assets

How to assess an asset's market value

Most people know that **assets** are what you own. Unfortunately, many people don't have a clear idea of everything they own—or how much those things are worth. Obviously, you're well aware of the bigger items you own—a car or a home, for example. But what about your books, your home office equipment, the china and silverware that you inherited, and those signed lithographs? You probably own more stuff than you realize.

Once you've listed all of your assets, you need to figure out how much each of those possessions is worth. How much money would you get, for example, if you cashed in your retirement plan? Or if you sold your home? Your furniture? Your coin collection? This dollar amount is known as market value. And it's easier to figure

for some assets than for others. Money in a checking account, for example, is worth exactly the amount written in your checkbook. But how much is your home worth, or your high-tech stocks? The **market value** of these types of assets varies over time—in some cases from day to day—so it's often hard to say just how much such an item is actually worth.

That's what makes net worth calculations so intimidating—and often prevents folks from doing it at all. "Dishwasher? TV? Home computer? I have no idea how much this stuff is worth!" Relax. The value you assign your baseball card collection doesn't have to be exact. For those hard-to-quantify assets, simply use a ballpark estimate. You can try searching online auctions, such as **www.eBay.com**, or calling an item's manufacturer if you really have no clue. But if you are really stuck, when we get to the worksheets, just leave the line blank for that asset for now and move on.

ASK THE EXPERTS

When calculating my assets, do I list the original price I paid for my expensive bike, or what it's worth now?

You want to know how much you would get if you sold that asset today—not what you spent on it in the first place. For some assets, such as a car, that can be a hard fact to accept. A car's value typically decreases over time, so even your one-year-old car is already worth less than what you bought it for. On the plus side, other assets, like houses, typically rise in value after being purchased.

On my assets worksheet, should I include possessions like my diamond wedding band, which I would never dream of selling?

It's probably a good idea. Many experts believe that you should add up every possession—including that diamond wedding band—because that will give the truest picture of your financial situation. Others feel that the point of a net worth calculation is to give you an idea of how much money you would have if you converted everything that you can sell to cash. Unless things are really dire, you're not going to sell your wedding band. However, if it's insured, that insurance would be worth something if the ring was stolen. Therefore, to be as accurate as possible in your calculations, it's best to include everything you own, within reason.

converting assets to cash

How easily can you get your hands on the money?

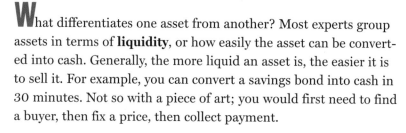

What differentiates one asset from another? Most experts group assets in terms of **liquidity**, or how easily the asset can be converted into cash. Generally, the more liquid an asset is, the easier it is to sell it. For example, you can convert a savings bond into cash in 30 minutes. Not so with a piece of art; you would first need to find a buyer, then fix a price, then collect payment.

Below are the five common asset groups, and instructions on how best to put a dollar figure on those assets. Review this information before filling out the Assets worksheet on the next page.

Cash This is money you can get your hands on easily, such as bank checking and savings accounts. Treasury bills and savings bonds also fall into this category, even if they have not reached their maturity date. For current values, check the most recent financial statement from your bank. For savings bonds, you can get current valuations at **www.treasurydirect.gov**.

Investments This group includes longer-term investments such as stocks, bonds, CDs, and mutual funds. (But don't include retirement assets in a 401(k) or IRA. This section includes only investments not tax-sheltered in retirement accounts.) You can find the current market value of these investments in the financial pages of major newspapers like the *Wall Street Journal* or the *New York Times*. Or you can call your broker or check your most recent brokerage statement. Also include the cash value of any life insurance policies. (That's the amount you'd get if you cashed in your policy now—not the policy's face value.) To obtain this value, call your insurance agent or write to the company that issued the policy.

Real Estate Any piece of real estate you own, such as your home, condominium, or co-op, as well as a second home or time-share, falls into this category. A home or apartment that you rent, however, should not be included. To determine your home's value, ask a local real estate agent for an estimate, use the real estate tax appraisal for your county, or check the newspaper or Internet (**www.realtor.com**) for listings of similar homes nearby.

Retirement Assets Your 401(k), IRA, and vested pension are all retirement assets. Check out your most recent IRA or 401(k) statement for the current value of your account, or check with your company's personnel department or the plan's sponsor. Pension plans are a bit tougher to value because so many variables affect the amount you receive. Still, your employer should be able to tell you what your pension would be worth if you retired now. This is known as your vested accrued pension benefit.

Personal Assets Your personal belongings, such as cars, furniture, and jewelry, fall into this category. Unfortunately, these are probably the toughest items to put a dollar figure on because their value depends on their condition and the current market demand for such products. Try to get an objective valuation whenever possible. If you have a coin collection, for example, contact an appraiser. To see how much your car is worth, look in the want ads for a similar make and model or get your car's "blue book" value from the *Kelley Blue Book Used Car Guide* (**www.kbb.com**). (Remember: Since you don't actually own leased cars, don't include them as assets.)

assets worksheet

Don't forget those antiquarian books or your time-share

In the worksheet on these two pages you'll find a space for nearly everything you own, from your used car and that treasured stamp collection to your vacation home at the shore. Not sure of an item's exact value? Don't sweat it. A rough estimate will do.

APPROXIMATE CURRENT VALUE

1. Cash Assets

Cash (in your wallet) _____

Checking account _____

Savings account _____

Money market account _____

Savings bonds _____

Treasury bills _____

Bonus (due soon, but not yet received) _____

Tax refund (due soon, but not yet received) _____

Other money you are owed _____

Other _____

    Total Cash Assets _____

2. Investment Assets

Certificates of deposit _____

Individual stocks _____

Stock mutual funds _____

Individual bonds _____

Bond mutual funds _____

Other mutual funds _____

Cash value of life insurance policies _____

Other _____

    Total Investment Assets _____

3. Real Estate Assets

Your home _____

Vacation home/second home	_____
Vacant land	_____
Time-share	_____
Other	_____
Total Real Estate Assets	_____
4. Retirement Assets	
401(k) plan, 403(b), or 457	_____
Traditional IRA	_____
SEP-IRA	_____
Roth IRA	_____
Keogh plan	_____
Vested pension plan	_____
Other	_____
Total Retirement Assets	_____
5. Personal Assets	
Vehicles	_____
Jewelry/furs/artwork/antiques	_____
Coin, stamp, or other collections	_____
Furniture	_____
Clothing	_____
Home appliances	_____
Home entertainment equipment	_____
Home office equipment	_____
Other	_____
Total Personal Assets	_____
Now its time to add it all up	
1. Cash Assets	_____
2. Investment Assets	_____
3. Real Estate Assets	_____
4. Retirement Assets	_____
5. Personal Assets	_____
YOUR TOTAL ASSETS	_____

understanding your liabilities

Putting a dollar value on your debts

The debts that you owe are called **liabilities**. For many people, that simply means the mortgage on the house and any outstanding school or car loans. But liabilities also include spousal or child support that you pay and taxes due to the IRS. Of course, if you regularly spend more than you earn, you might have some credit card debt, too.

In general, identifying your debts—and their value—is usually far easier than adding up your assets. Why? You probably have fewer debts than assets. And, in most cases, you don't have to guess how much debt you owe. Just look at your current bills or account statements for the actual figures. The current value for each of your debts is the **outstanding balance** of the loan. That's the original amount you borrowed, less any payments you have made. You don't need to include the total amount of the loan, when payment is due, or even the interest that you pay—just the outstanding balance that still has to be paid. With credit cards, you can simply check your most recent account statement for this amount. But with mortgages and many other types of loans, you may have to call (or write) the lender.

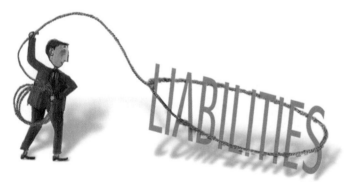

Work it out!

You'll find the Debt worksheet on the next page. But before you attempt to fill in the blanks, read the explanations below. They'll help you calculate the dollar value of your loans and other liabilities.

Home Mortgage. List the outstanding balance that you still owe on your mortgage (not the total amount that you originally borrowed). This information should be listed on your monthly statement or coupon payment book. If not, call your lender. Include similar information if you have a second home and/or a home equity loan.

Credit Card Debt. Use the outstanding balance from your last statement, or call the credit card company directly. Keep in mind, however, that your last statement may not reflect your most recent payments or new purchases. Also, don't forget to include the outstanding balances of all your credit cards—not just the largest balances. If you took out a home equity loan to consolidate your credit card debt, list that debt in the Mortgage Debt section (not here).

Education and Auto Loans. To see how much you still owe on these types of loans, check your monthly statements or your coupon payment books. If necessary, call the lender. One reminder: If you used a home equity loan to buy a car or to pay for tuition, list that loan under the Mortgage Debt section (not here).

Miscellaneous Debt. You'll probably have to call your insurer to get the balance due on a loan taken against your insurance policy. Ditto for a loan drawn from your 401(k) account. Unpaid taxes, however, may prove the most confusing. What should be included here? Capital gains taxes owed on investments, if a gain is realized; tax owed the IRS on April 15; and, if you're self-employed, your estimated quarterly taxes. Finally, include property taxes—if you're a homeowner and you pay those taxes yourself. (Many homeowners don't pay these taxes directly, however. The bank that holds their mortgage pays these taxes for them.)

debt worksheet

How much do you owe?

Itemizing your various debts—and the amount owed on each—isn't quite as much fun as toting up all those assets. But if you want an accurate net worth statement, you need to be as thorough with the liabilities side as you were with the assets.

	BALANCE	MONTHLY PAYMENT	INTEREST RATE
1. Mortage Debt			
Home mortgage	_____	_____	_____
Second mortgage	_____	_____	_____
Home equity loan	_____	_____	_____
Vacation or second home mortgage	_____	_____	_____
Total Mortage Debt	_____	_____	
2. Credit Card Debt			
Unpaid balances on all credit cards in your family:			
Card:_____	_____	_____	_____
Card:_____	_____	_____	_____
Card:_____	_____	_____	_____
Card:_____	_____	_____	_____
Card:_____	_____	_____	_____
Card:_____	_____	_____	_____
Total Credit Card Debt	_____	_____	
3. Vehicle Leases and Loans			
Auto loan 1	_____	_____	_____
Auto loan 2	_____	_____	_____
Auto lease 1	_____	_____	_____
Auto lease 2	_____	_____	_____
Boat loan	_____	_____	_____
Other vehicle loan	_____	_____	_____
Total Vehicle Debt	_____	_____	

	BALANCE	MONTHLY PAYMENT	INTEREST RATE
4. Educational Loans			
You	_____	_____	_____
Spouse	_____	_____	_____
Child	_____	_____	
Total Educational Loans	_____	_____	_____
5. Miscellaneous Debt			
Personal bank loans	_____	_____	_____
Loans from friends or family	_____	_____	_____
Home improvement loans	_____	_____	_____
Dental, medical, or hospital bills	_____	_____	_____
Unpaid taxes	_____	_____	_____
Money owed to the IRS	_____	_____	_____
Money borrowed against retirement account	_____	_____	_____
Money borrowed against life insurance policy	_____	_____	_____
Other	_____	_____	_____
Total Miscellaneous Debt	_____	_____	

Now it's time to add it all up.

	BALANCE	MONTHLY PAYMENT	
1. Mortgage Debt	_____	_____	
2. Credit Card Debt	_____	_____	
3. Vehicle Debt	_____	_____	
4. Educational Loans	_____	_____	
5. Miscellaneous Debt	_____	_____	
TOTAL LIABILITIES	_____	_____	

where do you stand?

A positive net worth means you have more assets than debts

Once you've filled in the worksheets, you can see how your assets and liabilities stack up. Find the total on your Debt worksheet (see page 81). Then, subtract that amount from the total on your Assets worksheet (see page 77). The result: your net worth.

$$\frac{\text{Total Assets}}{- \text{ Total Liabilities}}$$
$$= \textbf{Net Worth}$$

Chances are, if you are just starting out, your net worth will be a low number. What you want to know now is whether your net worth is positive or negative. A positive net worth means that you have more assets than debts. Congratulations! Having a positive net worth will make it easier to achieve your financial goals. And good budgeting will help you add to your net worth.

A negative net worth, on the other hand, means that you have too many debts and not enough savings. But its not the end of the world. Remember, you calculated your net worth to find out where you stand and work out a budget to improve your financial situation. Your goal now: to build more assets and pay off your debts. That will raise your net worth. When you are in the black again, it will be all that much easier to meet even bigger financial goals.

Sample NEGATIVE net worth

For a young couple that has just bought a house

Assets

Home	120,000
Checking account	1,200
401(k)	1,600
Vehicles	15,000
	137,800

Debts

Student loans	16,700
Car loan	13,000
Credit cards	1,300
Mortgage	113,000
	144,000

137,800 - 144,000= **$-6,200 Net Worth**

Sample POSITIVE net worth

For a widower about to retire

Assets

Home	185,000
401(k)/profit sharing	168,000
Vehicles	6,000
Raw land	25,000
Money market	20,000
Stock portfolio	48,000
	452,000

Debts

Mortgage	53,000

452,000 - 53,000= **$399,000 Net Worth**

ASK THE  EXPERTS

I make a good salary and own a home, but my net worth is lower than I expected. What changes should I make?

Look at your Assets Worksheet (pages 76-77). What types of assets do you own? What are your largest assets? Are they investment assets—such as a 401(k) or an IRA—or are they personal assets—such as furniture or jewelry? Investment assets offer the most long-term growth potential, so to improve your net worth, add more of these types of assets. Next, consider your liabilities. What types of debt do you have? How much interest do you pay? Could you take out a consolidation loan to lower your overall interest rate and pay debts off more quickly? Finally, check your variable and discretionary expenses (see Chapter 3) and see where you might be able to shave off a few dollars.

FIRST-PERSON SUCCESS STORY

A penny saved

When I landed my first job out of college, I immediately started putting $25 a month into a savings account. While all of my friends were using their every last penny on beach vacations and eating out, I was following the advice of my grandfather, who had retired with a large nest egg that had allowed him to live his last years in style. My friends made fun of me for being so tight-fisted, but I knew I'd be glad later. When I had saved $1,000, I put it into a long-term CD, and continued to do this over the years. I watched the interest add substantially to my original investments, and as these numbers went up, I diversified my portfolio by buying stocks and investing in mutual funds. The years have flown by, and now I'm about to retire myself. Thanks to my savings strategies, my financial house is in great order. Like my grandfather, after I retire I plan to travel far and wide and enjoy the good life. Most of the old friends who laughed at me back then are not in such great financial shape now—I bet they wish they'd given up a few of those dinners all those years ago and socked the money away like me.

—Larry B., St. Paul, MN

now what do I do?

Answers to common questions

How often should I calculate my net worth? When should I do it?

Financial experts typically recommend that you run your net worth numbers annually (at the beginning of the year, for example, so you can use the previous year's numbers) to see how you're doing. But you may find it easier to do your net worth calculations in April—after you've done your income taxes. That way, you will have many of the needed documents and figures already on hand. Another consideration: A good time to figure your net worth is when you're heading for a major milestone, like marriage, parenthood, or retirement, which may make added demands on your financial resources.

I know that my net worth should be positive and that it should increase over time. But by how much should it increase?

Good question. The answer depends on variables such as your time frame, your financial goals, and the types of assets you own. At the very least, your net worth should keep pace with inflation. Ideally, it should beat inflation. Over the past decade, inflation has been averaging a rather low 3% to 4% per year.

I tapped my savings to buy a home. Now my house is my biggest asset by far. Should I be concerned about liquidity?

Yes. Financial advisors suggest having a rainy day fund to tide you over in case of a financial emergency, such as losing your job. (See page 92.) This should be a liquid fund, meaning you can access it easily. In a worst case scenario, if you needed quick cash you could apply for a home equity loan on your home. However, it will take a few weeks before you'll have access to the money.

How can I raise my net worth?

You can raise your net worth in two basic ways. First, the assets that you already own can increase in value. For example: If the home that you bought five years ago is now worth $50,000 more than you originally paid for it, your net worth has increased. Second, you can use your current income to buy more assets or to pay down debt, cutting costly interest payments. Funneling extra cash into your retirement plan or paying off your entire credit card balance, for example, will increase your net worth. Most people typically use a combination of these tactics.

When estimating the current value of my home, do I need to subtract the standard 5% broker's commission from the price?

If you're being that precise with all of your valuations, then yes, go ahead and deduct the commission. But most people don't go to all this trouble.

Now where do I go?

Books

The Apple Pie Savings System
by Christopher S. Browning

Getting a Life: Strategies for Simple Living, Based on the Revolutionary Program for Financial Freedom, Your Money or Your Life
by Jacqueline Blix, David Heitmiller, Joseph R. Dominguez, and Joe Dominguez

The Motley Fool: You Have More than You Think: The Foolish Guide to Personal Finance
by David Gardner and Tom Gardner

50 Simple Things You Can Do to Improve Your Personal Finances: How to Spend Less, Save More, and Make the Most of What You Have
by Ilyce R. Glink

Web Sites

Yahoo! Real Estate
http://list.realestate.yahoo.com/re/homevalues
Analyze the value of your home or other homes by accessing public real estate records.

Understanding Your Finances
www.bygpub.com/finance
A series of helpful articles on personal money management, along with links to other finance sites.

Setting Goals

Chapter 5

"We find it easier to save with a goal in mind."

identifying your goals

Ask yourself what you want

Great, the hard part is over: You've calculated your cash flow and found out your net worth. Well done! Now comes the fun part: setting your **financial goals**. In fact, budgeting without a clearly defined goal usually doesn't work.

Financial goals will vary, naturally, from one person to the next. And at different times in your life, your goals will change depending on your needs. When you're younger, you'll probably be more concerned about having a baby or buying a home than with retirement or long-term care insurance. Whatever your individual goals, though, they can all be divided into three categories: short-term, medium-term, and long-term.

1. Short-term goals are things you want to do soon, such as buy a new TV next month, take a vacation, or pay down credit card debt. Generally, short-term goals require immediate attention and are accomplished within a year or two.

2. Medium-term goals are things that take a bit more time—generally, about five years—such as putting a down payment on a home, saving up to have a baby, or taking a trip abroad.

3. Long-term goals take far longer—more than 10 years, in most cases—to achieve. Funding a retirement nest egg, buying a vacation home, or starting your own business are long-term goals that many folks strive for.

Some typical goals

- Renovate home
- Save for gifts
- Buy life insurance
- Pay off credit cards
- Contribute to 401K/IRA
- Build a retirement fund
- Build a long-term care fund
- Build a pool/deck
- Pay off college loans
- Buy a vacation home
- Take time off work
- Change careers
- Start a business

Goals that keep on giving

One important thing to keep in mind as you start setting financial goals is that not all goals are created equal. Some goals give back over time by increasing your equity, while with others, the money you save—and then spend—does not improve your net worth or wealth in any way. There are three kinds of goals:

1. Goals that give back over time

These are goals that improve your net worth or earning power over time. For example, saving to pay for a college education is smart because it will enable you to command a higher salary later on. And buying a house or starting a retirement fund will give you equity you can borrow against to purchase other assets, not to mention it can help fund a comfortable lifestyle in your golden years.

2. Goals that break even

Renovating your home or buying a car are goals that keep you on an even keel. The money you save up to renovate your home will hopefully be offset by the rise in your home's value over time, or such improvements could even improve your current net worth if the renovations result in a dramatic increase in your home's value. Likewise, the money you spend on a new car could be offset by the money you'll save by not taking public transportation, or by the higher salary you can earn by being able to commute to a job in another city.

3. Fun goals

These kinds of goals do not provide you with any kind of financial gain. Once you save up for this goal and spend the money, it's gone. Examples of fun goals are an extravagant vacation, an expensive outfit, or a fancy party. Be sparing with these kinds of goals, and make sure you always have some "value-added" goals as well (the first kind of goal).

FIRST-PERSON DISASTER STORY

Savings stumble

About five years ago my brother and I decided to start saving money to buy a beach house for our families to share. However, we never bothered to draw up specific financial goals and never did any research to see how much money we would need for a down payment. We just plunked any extra cash—and often it was just a small amount—into a catchall account. As long as we were saving something every month, we figured we would come out ahead. We finally checked the account last week and realized we had nowhere near the amount we needed for a down payment. I wish we had set goals beforehand and figured out just how much we needed to save! I also wish we'd put the money into a savings plan with a higher interest rate. If we had, we probably could have been enjoying our beach house today!

—Amy C., Bethesda, MD

getting out of debt

When your most important goal is getting out of the red

One of the most fundamental financial goals that many people have is getting out of debt. As unexciting as it sounds, this is the first step to building real financial security. Once you have your debt under control, then you can start thinking about fun financial goals, such as saving for that Caribbean vacation, and goals that give back over time, like retirement savings.

Getting out of debt does not necessarily mean paying every cent you owe. For most folks, this is simply impossible—especially if they have a mortgage. What it does mean is paying off as many debts as possible, starting with those that have the highest interest rates (such as credit cards). It also means settling any delinquent debts to prevent further damage to your credit report and to get creditors off your back. This is where a **debt consolidation loan** might help. (See next page.)

If getting completely out of debt is impossible because you have a mortgage or other major debt (such as student loans for medical school), concentrate on reducing your debt to a level you can live with. According to financial experts, your total debt should be less than 25% of your annual salary—although this varies depending on your age, income, total assets, and total liabilities.

However, if your debt consists of a few credit card balances, a car loan, and perhaps a small bank loan, then paying off all of your debt in the next few years should be a reasonable goal. But in this case, you need to make sure you don't add new debt as you pay off your old debt, or you won't get anywhere. This means putting your credit cards in deep freeze, passing up a new car loan and paying cash for a decent used car, and being aware of all the other debt traps you can fall into—then avoiding them.

Just as with any other financial goal, if your goal is to get out of debt, you need to settle on the amount you want to apply toward your debts, give yourself a deadline, and then save a set amount every month. With a little determination, you'll probably be able to wipe your debt slate clean much sooner than you expected.

Debt-free retirement

It's a good idea to get out of debt before you retire. Living on a fixed income after retiring can be a strain, creating even more temptation to abuse your credit cards. Ideally, while you're still young, you should also start socking away some of your savings in tax-deferred retirement plans (see pages 180-181), to ensure that your golden years are comfortable and worry-free.

ASK THE EXPERTS

I am drowning in credit card and student loan debt. How do I get a debt consolidation loan to pay it all off? How much can I get?

First, sit down and figure out how much you owe altogether, then go to your bank and talk to a loan officer. Assuming your credit is acceptable, the bank will loan you a lump sum of money that you can use to pay off your credit cards and other high-interest debts. Keep in mind that you must begin paying back the loan immediately, with interest, in agreed-upon monthly installments. Typically, however, the bank's interest rate and fees should be lower than your credit card interest, so you can end up saving a lot of money.

The amount the bank will loan you depends on your income. Usually, a bank assumes that you will be able to put aside up to 36% of your gross income (before taxes) to pay your debt. So, if your salary is $45,000, the bank will assume you could use up to $18,000 of your annual net income for loan payments. That's the amount the bank will probably loan you (unless they subtract existing debts, such as a mortgage or car loan, out of your gross salary before calculating that 36%, in which case the amount of your loan will be lower).

If I get a debt consolidation loan, isn't this just going to put me deeper in debt?

Not necessarily. While at first glance, going deeper into debt seems like the last thing you would want to do, it actually makes a lot of sense to get a debt consolidation loan—but only if you can borrow the money at a lower interest rate than what you are paying on your other debts, and only if you stop racking up new debt in the meantime.

Is it better to pay off my credit cards first before I start putting money into my company's 401(k) plan?

Many experts suggest that you do both at the same time. Enroll in the 401(k) as soon as possible, up to the amount the company will match (assuming there is a match), then apply all surplus cash flow toward knocking down your credit card debt as soon as possible.

your emergency fund

You need a cash reserve...just in case

There's one financial goal that should be a high priority on everyone's list: building an **emergency cash fund**. This money will help cover the costs of those unexpected rainy days, such as when you lose your job, the roof starts leaking, or you are seriously hurt in an accident. An emergency fund is a financial safety net. It gives you peace of mind, and it means that you won't have to stop saving for your other goals—or worse, reach for those credit cards and go into debt—when a crisis arises.

Most financial experts recommend that you set aside three to six months' income. For most people, that's enough money to repair a problem or to cover their living expenses if they are out of work for a while. This money should be kept separate from other savings. Don't lump it in with college savings, retirement savings, or even your regular checking account. If the funds are not kept separate, you might be tempted—or simply forget—and use the money for a non-emergency. (Also, there are tax consequences if you take retirement money out early.) In addition, an emergency fund should be liquid because you may need to get your hands on that cash quickly. But just because the fund is liquid, don't get into it unless it truly is an emergency.

Finally, your emergency cash should be stashed in a super-safe investment. Consider:

- regular savings accounts

- CDs—certificates of deposit (see page 182)

- money market accounts, available at your bank (see page 182)

- money market mutual fund accounts, available from mutual fund companies (see page 182)

- U.S. Treasury securities (see page 183). However, these are not the most practical option unless they have passed their maturity date and you can withdraw them without penalty.

ASK THE  EXPERTS

I don't have an emergency fund. Should I set aside that money first—and then start saving for retirement?

Not necessarily. While some people like to save for one goal at a time, many folks save for various goals simultaneously. In most cases, it makes good financial sense to do so. Simply decide how much you can afford to save each month. Then divide that sum among your various short-, medium-, and long-term goals. (An emergency fund is a short-term goal.) It may take you longer to build your emergency account this way, but, as you build up your cash reserve, you'll also be taking advantage of long-term, tax-deferred growth through your retirement savings.

What happens if an emergency hits before I've accumulated enough money?

You may have to borrow the needed funds. Two popular and relatively cheap options include borrowing against the cash value of your life insurance and borrowing against your 401(k). If you're a homeowner, consider taking a loan against your house. The advantage: You can arrange for this loan in advance so that the money is available should you need it with a home equity line of credit. Here's how it works: You take out a home equity line of credit for up to 80% of your home's value, minus your mortgage balance. Once the paperwork is filed, the bank hands you a checkbook, instead of a lump sum payment. When you need money, you can write yourself a check (up to the determined amount). You pay no interest until you actually use it. And the interest paid is generally tax-deductible, as long as the second mortgage is less than $100,000.

saving for a wedding

Paying for the biggest party of your life

If one of your main financial goals is to save for a wedding, the first thing you need to do is decide what you are willing and able to pay for. There are many options for paying for weddings: Some folks follow the tradition of having the bride's family pay for nearly everything, while some couples prefer to pay for everything themselves. Because there are so many possibilities, having this conversation with your family and your fiancé's family early on can prevent a lot of misunderstanding.

Once that is decided, the second thing you need to do is create a budget. The desire for an unforgettable celebration will have to be balanced with the reality of what you can actually afford. If the wedding or honeymoon of your dreams is out of reach because of a lack of funds, do not apply for a loan. Beginning your marriage under a pile of debt is never a good idea, since it will surely become a source of tension in the future. Your best bet is to wait until you've saved enough for the wedding that you want, and then cut costs where you can. And check wedding Web sites (such as **www.theknot.com**) for tips on cutting wedding costs without sacrificing elegance.

After you've set your budget, divide that number by the total number of months you have to save for the event. But make sure you have access to the bulk of those savings at least six months before the wedding, because you will need to start putting down deposits for wedding-service providers. Whenever possible, use your credit card for these deposits because if something goes wrong (say, the florist never shows up), you can simply contact your credit card company and they may be able to have your deposit refunded. Charging purchases on your credit cards—and paying them off—will also help you build your credit. Plus, if your card offers rewards for each dollar spent, you can end up sitting pretty: Many couples earn enough frequent-flier miles to convert into free airline tickets for a second honeymoon.

Wedding insurance

A wedding can be a huge expense. You may wish to purchase insurance for your wedding. Policies generally cover cancellation or postponement of the event, as well as loss coverage for photography and videography, wedding attire, gifts, rings, and deposits. Call your insurance agent for details, or contact WedSafe (www.wedsafe.com, 1-877-SAFE-WED), or the Fireman's Fund (www.firemansfund.com, 1-800-ENGAGE).

Wedding budgeting

Okay, you've established a budget limit for your wedding. Now, find the column below that matches your budget and see how these resources are usually allocated to pay for the many different elements of a wedding. (Note: Prices vary from region to region.)

CATEGORY	% of Budget	$10,000 Budget	$20,000 Budget	$30,000 Budget
Food & Beverages	30%	$3,000	$6,000	$9,000
Attire	10%	$1,000	$2,000	$3,000
Site Fees	10%	$1,000	$2,000	$3,000
Photography & Videography	10%	$1,000	$2,000	$3,000
Flowers & Decor	10%	$1,000	$2,000	$3,000
Music & Entertainment	10%	$1,000	$2,000	$3,000
Transportation	8%	$500	$1,600	$2,400
Miscellaneous	5%	$500	$1,000	$1,500
Gifts & Favors	5%	$500	$1,000	$1,500
Stationery	2%	$200	$400	$600

Depending on the size of your budget, you can probably cut back in certain categories to give you more money to spend in a different category. For example, if you have a $10,000 budget but you choose not to rent a limousine, that can yield you a savings of 8% right off the top. Those savings can go toward another category that you'd prefer to focus on, such as site fees, if you want to have your wedding at a posh, private resort. Or you might prefer to put that extra money toward your honeymoon or toward the down payment on a home.

your dream home

Putting a roof over your head without breaking the bank

If your goal is to buy a home, the first thing you need to do is figure out how much house you can afford. Unless you are fabulously wealthy and plan to pay for your home in cash, you will probably need to take out a mortgage and make monthly payments on it for many years. So, in calculating what you can pay for a house, you need to take into account the maximum monthly housing costs you can comfortably afford (and then you may choose to buy smaller!). Lenders will want you to borrow as much as you qualify for, but that may be more than you can afford to pay each month.

Here's a simple rule to help you determine what you can afford to borrow. In general, your projected monthly housing costs (including mortgage payments, property taxes, and insurance) shouldn't exceed 28% of your gross monthly income. (Gross is your total income before any deductions for taxes.) These costs, plus your other long-term debt payments (like car loans, credit card payments, and student loans) should not exceed 36% of your gross monthly income.

Once you have come up with a reasonable estimate of how much house you can afford, you need to put away about 20% of that estimate for a down payment. If you can't muster that much, you'll have to pay for private mortgage insurance, which protects the bank in case you can't make your payments. If you can't afford the down payment but earn enough to afford monthly payments, check out government-backed loans from Fannie Mae, 1 (800) 732-6643, **www.fanniemae.com**; or the Federal Housing Administration, 1 (800) 483-7342, **www.hud.gov/fha**.

In addition, heaped on the down payment like meatballs on spaghetti will be one-time fees and closing costs, to the tune of about 2% to 5% of the amount of your mortgage.

A financial planner (see pages 24-25) can help you work out these figures and set up a savings strategy so that you'll wind up in a new house, rather than the poorhouse.

ASK THE  EXPERTS

Everybody keeps telling me, "Don't forget to put aside some money for closing fees." What are these exactly?

Closing fees are the various costs you will need to pay when you close on the sale of a house. These costs typically include the following:

- Application Fee. The lender charges a fee to process your loan application.

- Legal Fees. These are fees paid to your real estate lawyer to review your purchasing contract and deed.

- Points. This is the fee that the lender charges the borrower to arrange the mortgage. One point equals one percent of the amount you borrow. (If your credit is good and interest rates are already low, you shouldn't have to pay any points.)

- Inspection Fee. The lender will want to know that the home isn't infested with termites before giving you a loan to buy it. You need to pay a house inspector to check out your future home.

- Appraisal Fee. Is the house worth more than the amount you want to borrow? An appraiser can help you find out.

- Title Insurance Fee. You need to have the title to your future home checked for liens—claims on it by contractors or previous owners.

- Credit Check. The lender will need to see if you are creditworthy.

I've finally saved up enough to buy a house. Now, how do I find a low mortgage rate?

Start by finding out what the competitive rates are at **www.bankrate.com**. Then, start calling banks, mortgage companies, and mortgage brokers, or visiting sites such as **www.loanworks.com** and **www.eloan.com** to see what they can offer. Ask for the APR, or annual percentage rate, to compare the real cost of a loan from lender to lender. The APR includes interest plus fees and points (see above). Then ask your local banker if he can match or beat a competitor's rates, or, at the very least, waive fees or point charges.

a new baby

Why costs soar when the stork pays you a visit

So you're going to have a baby! Congratulations! As excited as you are, you probably also know that along with those adorable smiles will come a steady stream of bills—for at least 18 years. So, the sooner you can start putting money aside to fund the new arrival, the better shape you'll be in once Junior has arrived.

What kinds of costs can you expect? Even before the baby arrives, there's the obstetrician's bill, which ranges from $2,000 to $6,000. Then there's the hospital bill and the pediatrician's bill. By the time your bundle is ready to go home, you could be handed bills totalling around $8,000. That's why, before you even get to the baby-planning stages, it's a good idea to check your health insurance policy to see exactly what it does and does not cover, then start saving accordingly.

Many people mistakenly assume that the birth itself is the most expensive baby-related cost, and they think that a baby doesn't eat much or need many things. However, figures from the U.S. Department of Agriculture (USDA) show that, as of 1999, the average family spends about $9,420 a year to raise a child—a total of about $160,140 from birth to age 17. And that doesn't include paying for college!

Almost a third of that USDA estimate goes toward the bigger house or apartment you will need. But there is still another $6,280 in other expenses: A baby uses about $1,000 of infant food each year, $450 in clothing, $560 in health care, and $1,200 in medical care, diapers, and supplies.

What to do? The best way to manage these costs is to try and save for the expense of children before you have them. If you are in the family frame of mind, start rethinking your monthly expenses. Maybe forgo expensive entertainment items or put off a vacation. In other words, you may need to scale back now, and certainly after your bundle of joy arrives, to accommodate baby's needs now and in the future. Go through the baby fiscal checklist on the next page to find other ways to cut costs.

New baby financial checklist

Sound fiscal planning doesn't end with Junior's birth. There are many other things you can do to keep your fiscal house in order after baby makes three . . . or four, or five:

1. Get your child a social security number. Usually you fill out the form in the hospital, but if you didn't, call Social Security at 1 (800) 772-1213 or visit the Web site at **www.ssa.gov** and get the form. Once you have your baby's Social Security number, as of this writing you can list him as a personal deduction and cut $1,000 off your taxes. (In the old days, you didn't need a Social Security number to claim a child, but now you do.)

2. Review your insurance. Before kids it was just you and your spouse. Now you need to factor in the needs of a child for at least 18 years, more if you want to include college. Make sure you have enough life insurance to cover baby's needs as well as your spouse's. Review your disability policy and increase it if necessary.

3. Check your will. If you don't have a will, draft one. If you have a will, revise it to include your new heir. This is grim, but necessary: You need to name legal guardians for all your minor children, should you and your spouse die unexpectedly.

4. Review your investment beneficiaries. Check all investments, such as your life insurance and retirement plans, that allow you to list **beneficiaries**, the people who get the proceeds from your investments when you die. Prior to having a baby, you probably listed your spouse as your primary beneficiary. It's smart to have the guardian of your children listed as a secondary beneficiary to make sure your children get the money in the event you and your spouse pass away simultaneously.

5. Start a college fund early. If you can muster the strength and discretionary income to open an account now, the wonder of compounding interest will reward you later. See page 103 for types of funds.

6. Organize your files along with all those baby albums. And keep a financial file for baby, so that vital financial papers can be found quickly if there is an emergency.

brand new wheels

A practical approach to car buying

So you have your heart set on a new car? As with buying a house, you won't be expected to pay for the whole thing up front. In most cases, however, you will need to save up the down payment. This is usually at least 10% of the car's price, though this may be less if you trade in your existing car. Doing your homework ahead of time so you know what you can expect to pay, then making a smart decision when it comes to leasing or buying, new or used, can save you money down the road.

A lease is usually the best bet if you like to trade in your car every couple of years. Some leases don't require a down payment; instead, you pay a set monthly amount. At the end of the lease, you return the car and owe nothing, or you can buy the car. However, if you have enough money for the down payment, or plan to keep a car for more than a few years, or drive more than 15,000 miles per year, then buying is better.

One of the best ways to save money is to buy or lease a solid used car that's at least two or three years old, instead of buying a new one. The down payment, monthly payments, and insurance are often substantially less for a used car. Not to mention, a new car's value drops by 10% when you drive it off the lot. For this reason, think twice before your sink your savings into a new car.

Whether you decide to buy or lease, you can also save loads if you negotiate the price. The sticker price does not reflect the rock-bottom price that the dealer will accept, so bargain hard. But before you do, investigate online. Check out new and used car prices at **www.carpoint.com**, **www.autoworld.com**, *Kelley Blue Book* (**www.kbb.com**), or the *Official Used Car Guide of the National Automobile Dealers Association* (**www.nada.org**).

Once you learn the true cost of the car you want to buy, call around to dealers and start bidding. If a dealer doesn't cooperate, then scratch that dealer from your list.

With these savvy strategies, getting a new set of wheels will cost you much less than you thought.

> ### Hidden car costs
>
> The average cost of a new car is $25,800. But whether you buy or lease, it's not only car payments you have to come up with. The American Automobile Association has estimated that motorists who drive 15,000 miles a year pile on $7,363 more in car-related expenses, including insurance costs and personal property taxes.

Smart car savings

Here are some additional ways to save when it comes to getting a new car:

1. As you look at makes and manufacturers, consider a new electric hybrid car or one that uses an alternative fuel source. Not only are these cars much cheaper to operate in the long run, they are much better for the environment. And some models allow you to take a tax credit.

2. Start at the low end of your budget and work your way to the car of your choice. It's too hard to go from looking at $35,000 vehicles to making do with a $22,000 one.

3. Try to get preapproved for a car loan before you go shopping. It's better to know up front how much you can borrow and what the terms are before you lose your senses over that new-car smell. Talk to your bank to see what they can do for you. Also check with several car dealers to see what kinds of loan terms they offer.

4. Learn about the current range of interest rates on new- and used-car loans. Check out the national averages at **www.bankrate.com**.

5. When you're working out the total cost and payment terms with the dealer, remember that getting a low interest rate and a shorter repayment period is more important than having a low monthly payment.

6. Ask your banker or car dealer about taking out a simple-interest loan instead of an installment loan (also called a front-end loan). With a simple-interest loan, you pay interest only on the remaining principal. With an installment loan, you pay interest on the entire principal throughout the term of the loan. This means that even if, for example, you have paid $8,000 on a $15,000 installment loan, you will continue to pay interest on the entire $15,000!

7. You can take out a home equity loan to finance your car if you are a homeowner and have enough equity. The rate may be cheaper, and the interest you pay is usually tax deductible.

paying for college

Planning ahead for the cost of a diploma

You've decided you want to go to college or perhaps finish your degree. What a great idea.

What you need to do at this point is look at what kind of education your income can support, then start saving accordingly. And also consider ways to cut college costs. For example, keep in mind that there are many excellent state universities, as well as community colleges, that offer a fine selection of courses and a respected degree. Plus, the extra earning power you might have with an Ivy-League degree may not really compensate for the fact that it costs twice as much to go there as a good state school.

If your budget won't allow for a pricey private school, think about enrolling in a less expensive community college for the first two years. This will give you time to add to your college fund. Then, you can transfer to a more prestigious school for the last two years. Or, trim down the number of semesters you have to pay for at an expensive college by supplementing with credits taken at a less expensive college during the summer. (Just make sure the tuition credits are transferable.)

And remember, if you have a modest income and can't save all the funds you'll need (and most people can't), you may qualify for aid or grants. If you have a high salary but many other expenses, you may be able to take out loans. You can also withdraw from your traditional or Roth IRA (see page 180) to pay for college expenses, but consider this option carefully before doing it. And yes, it's worth it, even if you have to borrow to do it: College grads earn twice the annual salary of high school grads!

College costs

Projected average annual cost of a private college, including room and board:

2003: $25,586

2004: $26,866

2005: $28,209

2006: $29,620

2007: $31,100

Add about a third if your child has her sights set on an Ivy League school, and subtract about a third if your child plans on attending the local state university or a public school.

Source: The Princeton Review

ASK THE  EXPERTS

I know I won't be able to pay for my son's entire college education. What kind of financial aid options are out there?

There are three options when it comes to financial aid for college. When your son applies to college, you will complete a FAFSA (Free Application for Federal Student Aid), which will determine your eligibility for various kinds of aid, such as the following:

- **Grants and scholarships** These are awards made to students which do not have to be paid back. They vary in amount and are given by the federal government (known as Pell Grants), by state governments, by the colleges themselves, and by private organizations.

- **Loans** A number of federally supported loans are available to college students and to their parents. You will have to pay these back someday, but the interest rate on college loans is much lower than it is for bank loans.

- **Work-study** This is a federal program that matches students with part-time on-campus jobs. Student typically use the money they earn to cover minor expenses, such as books and clothing.

College savings plans

If you are saving for college, consider putting the money into one of these special educational savings plans:

Coverdell Education Savings Account This allows you to put away up to $2,000 per year per child; the interest you earn is tax free if the savings are used to pay for college.

529 plan This is a state-managed fund in which you can save up to $180,000-$305,000 (the amount depends on the state). The money you earn compounds tax-free, and you are usually not taxed when you withdraw it either. The savings can be used to pay for the college of your choice.

Visit **www.savingforcollege.com** or **www.collegesavings.org** for more information about saving for college.

prioritizing your goals

Decide what's most important to you

Great! You've identified your financial goals—and you've calculated how much those goals will cost and how long it will take you. Now it's time to sharpen those No. 2 pencils and draw up a workable plan. After you get a grip on what you need to save, in the next chapter you will learn how to create a budget to help you reach these goals.

Here are step-by-step directions for filling in the Financial Goals worksheet on pages 106-107.

Step #1
Begin by listing your goals, each one as short-, medium- or long-term. List as many goals as you can. This is your wish list.

Step #2
Fill in the approximate total cost of each goal (see the box at right). This will require you to do some legwork—either by shopping around, calling friends, or reading up on the costs of, say, that trip to Disneyworld. But putting in the effort will pay off: Having a dollar figure on a goal makes it real. It's no longer just a dream.

Step #3
Next, jot down when you hope to reach each goal. Dates for some goals, such as saving for holiday gifts or taking a summer vacation, will be relatively easy to determine. Others are much more flexible. Let's say that you want to buy new living room furniture. Do you need that sofa and love seat in four months? Or could you make do with your old futon couch for a year?

Step #4
Find out how much you need to set aside each month to reach your goal. Fill this in under "Amount to be saved per month." For many short- and medium-term goals, you can simply divide the amount needed by your time frame. If you need $1,000 for a new TV, for example, and you hope to buy it in 10 months, then you need to save $100 per month. The more time you have to save, the less you'll need to save each month.

Step #5

Finally, rank your goals according to importance. Which goal is a must-have? Which goal can wait for another year? Perhaps the toughest part of this exercise, this task means accepting the fact that you can't have it all at the same time. While there are no hard and fast goal-setting rules, of course, you probably can't save for more than one or two goals in each category at the same time. In fact, limiting yourself to just three or four goals total will probably increase the likelihood that you'll not only achieve them, but that you'll do it within a reasonable amount of time. Once you've secured those top priority items, you can then look to items further down the list.

The real cost of your goals

The cost of most things doesn't remain stable over time. Prices go up—thanks to inflation. How will this affect how you price your goals? For short-term goals, inflation isn't really an issue. The amount you determine to save today for furniture you won't actually buy for another 18 months will not be affected. (Not by much, anyway.)

Medium- and long-term goals are different. Let's say you are saving to put a down payment on a house in five years. Using today's prices, you figure you need $15,000. Over those five years that you'll be saving, though, housing prices may rise sharply. At the end of your five-year saving period, you may discover that the down payment needed is now $20,000. You will have reached your original goal, yet you still won't have enough money for a down payment on a house.

To guard against this situation, you may want to factor in inflation when calculating the cost of your goals. This isn't quite as complicated or confusing as it sounds—even for those among us who are severely math-challenged! Simply scan the financial pages of the newspaper or listen to the news on TV for an inflation forecast. (Financial experts love to forecast the rate of inflation.) Take that number—let's say it's 5% annually—and multiply it by the current cost of your goal. Add the result to the current cost. Repeat for every year that you need to reach your goal. The result is your inflation-adjusted price.

financial goals worksheet

A goal is a dream with a deadline

See the directions on the preceding page to fill out this worksheet.

SHORT-TERM GOALS	Amount Needed	Amount to Be Saved Per Month	Date Wanted	Rank in Importance
Build an emergency cash fund	_____	_____	_____	_____
Eliminate credit card debt	_____	_____	_____	_____
Take a vacation	_____	_____	_____	_____
Save (in advance) for Christmas gifts	_____	_____	_____	_____
Make home repairs	_____	_____	_____	_____
Renovate home	_____	_____	_____	_____
Make a large purchase (furniture, household appliances, electronic equipment, etc.)	_____	_____	_____	_____
Buy life insurance	_____	_____	_____	_____
Start a savings plan	_____	_____	_____	_____
Other	_____	_____	_____	_____
Total short-term goals	_____	_____		

MEDIUM-TERM GOALS	Amount Needed	Amount to Be Saved Per Month	Date Wanted	Rank in Importance
Contribute maximum to 401(k) plan and/or IRA	_____	_____	_____	_____
Put a down payment on a home	_____	_____	_____	_____
Take a dream vacation	_____	_____	_____	_____
Have a baby	_____	_____	_____	_____
Buy a new car	_____	_____	_____	_____
Pay off college loan	_____	_____	_____	_____
Throw a big party (wedding, sweet 16, bar mitzvah, etc.)	_____	_____	_____	_____
Other	_____	_____	_____	_____
Total medium-term goals	_____	_____		

financial goals worksheet cont'd

LONG-TERM GOALS	Amount Needed	Amount to Be Saved Per Month	Date Wanted	Rank in Importance
Fund retirement nest egg	_____	_____	_____	_____
Buy a vacation home	_____	_____	_____	_____
Start your own business	_____	_____	_____	_____
Send the kids to college	_____	_____	_____	_____
Go back to school	_____	_____	_____	_____
Buy long-term care insurance	_____	_____	_____	_____
Travel extensively	_____	_____	_____	_____
Other	_____	_____	_____	_____
Total long-term goals	_____	_____		

ALL GOALS	Amount Needed	Amount to Be Saved Per Month
Short-term	_____	_____
Medium-term	_____	_____
Long-term	_____	_____
Total goals	_____	_____

ASK THE EXPERTS

I really want to save for a new car, but I'm worried that I'm going to forget to put money away every month, or that I'll spend my whole paycheck beforehand. Any tips?

It bears repeating the single most important piece of advice that most financial experts agree on: Pay yourself first. This means that when you get your paycheck, immediately put aside the amount you've decided to save monthly toward your goal. Do this before you pay any of your bills or other expenses. This way, you'll never find yourself in the position of spending your entire paycheck before setting aside what you've promised yourself to save every month.

If, however, the hard part is not scraping the money together, but remembering to pay yourself first, take the responsibility out of your hands by setting up an automatic investment plan with your bank. A set amount of money will be deducted every month from your paycheck and deposited into a savings or money market account. See page 184 for more information.

I'm saving for three goals at the same time. What's the best way to keep track of how well I'm doing?

Simple. Turn to the back of your spending or budgeting diary and set aside a page for each of your goals. At the top of each page, write the name of the goal and the type of savings strategy you are using to reach it (e.g., money market account, bonds, etc.). Then, list all the months (and years) you are giving yourself to reach this goal, one month per line. Every month, write down how much you have saved toward your goal next to the month's name. Keep a running tally, too. Personal budgeting software can also be set up to track this for you. Then, when you need a little encouragement, just take a look at these pages and see how well you're doing!

now what do I do?

Answers to common questions

Why is it so important to have financial goals? Can't I just create a budget and decide how to spend the money later?

Sure. But having goals can really help you understand why you're saving. A specific goal—complete with a price tag and the savings commitment you'll make each month—acts as a beacon, guiding your spending and saving efforts. Without clearly defined goals, you may lose your incentive to save. It's far too tempting to use spare cash for other, more immediate purchases. Finally, you need to know where you're headed—that's what goals help you determine—before you can map out a plan to get there.

I have a long list of items I'd like to buy. Do I include these in my list of goals?

No. Relatively small items like a leather jacket or a new mountain bike that you hope to buy when you have some extra cash on hand are "wants" rather than goals. (Typically, this extra cash is left over after you pay your bills and put money aside for savings.) Goals, on the other hand, are bigger-ticket items, such as a home, a car, or a vacation, that you must save for over time. See page 120 for more on how to set aside some "fun" money for these occasional splurges without killing your budget.

Which should we save for first, remodeling the kitchen or a luxury vacation?

Ideally, you should prioritize the goal that offers a higher return on your hard-earned investment. A remodeled kitchen will add resale value to your home, while a vacation will not provide you with any financial return. This doesn't mean you should forget about saving for a vacation, but it does mean that ranking a remodel above a vacation is probably a wise idea. And don't forget that with some extra effort, it is possible to save for more than one financial goal at a time.

I would love to start saving to buy a house. But can I do this while I'm still deep in credit card debt?

Yes, you can. It just means you'll have to create an extra-strict budget that will help you pay off your credit card debt and start saving toward a down payment on a house. And, because you are saving toward two goals, it may take you a bit longer. Ideally, you want to have your credit card debt paid off before you buy your house, though it's not absolutely necessary. Just make sure that you don't sign up for a mortgage while you're still deep in credit card debt, or you will end up in an even tighter bind.

Now where do I go?

Books

The Road to Wealth: A Comprehensive Guide to Your Money—Everything You Need to Know in Good and Bad Times
by Suze Orman

The Truth About Money
by Ric Edelman

Making the Most of Your Money
by Jane Bryant Quinn

Rich Dad, Poor Dad: What the Rich Teach Their Kids About Money That the Poor and Middle Class Do Not
by Robert T. Kiyosaki with Sharon L. Lechter, CPA

Web Sites

Try these calculators to figure out the real costs of your goals:

Calcbuilder
www.calcbuilder.com
You'll find calculators for retirement, college planning, budgeting, auto loans, and mortgages.

Smart Money Magazine
www.smartmoney.com
Use the college planning worksheet here to help you figure out how much to save through 529 college savings plans.

CNN and Money Magazine
http://money.cnn.com
You'll find calculators for retirement, college savings, and debt reduction.

Kiplinger's
www.kiplinger.com
There are calculators for just about everything:

■ Investing: How much risk can I take? How much difference will the rate make?

■ Credit: What will it take to pay off my balance?

■ Home: How much can I spend for housing?

■ Saving: What will it take for me to become a millionaire someday?

Your Budget in Action

CHAPTER 6

**"This is the first time
I've ever had a
realistic plan
for my money."**

the big picture

Get ready, get set—and save!

Congratulations! The hard part—tracking all those annoying expenses—is over. Now you need to take what you've learned about your spending patterns, pair it with your financial goals, and come up with a realistic budget that will get you where you want to go.

Relax. You can—and will—get that spending under control. That was the point, after all, of tracking your expenses: to see where the money actually went. Now you know. Until now, you may not have realized that you were spending so much. Most people don't. That's because overspending doesn't just happen. It rises slowly and steadily, along with your income, until one day—this day—you see the problem and decide to fix it.

The solution, of course, is a budget. Not one of those bare-bones, save-$100-a-day-or-bust budgets, but a realistic spending plan that will guide you, like a good road map, safely toward your financial goals—in a style that you can live with. Contrary to what you you may have heard or read in the past, a budget is not a diet. Rather, it's a plan that lets you take control of your money. It helps you get where you want to be.

Before you get started on the road to Budgetville, take a look at where you are. If you have a **negative cash flow**—that is, you're spending more than you earn—your first job is to break even. You want your expenses to equal your income, not exceed them. If you're already at the break-even point, then you'll want to tweak your expenses to free up some cash. Without doing this, you won't be able to save to meet your financial goals. Even if you already have some extra cash left over after all the bills are paid, it's still a good idea to examine your expenses to eliminate wasteful or unnecessary spending. No matter how much you spend or earn, you always want to get the most value for your money.

Setting budget guidelines

Now that you've tracked your expenses for a while, it's time to analyze the information you've collected and set some reasonable budget guidelines.

Looking over your spending diary, what kinds of patterns emerge? You are probably surprised to see how much money you've been spending on entertainment, eating out, and "miscellaneous." According to financial experts, these are the top three money leaks for most people.

Your goal is to stop those leaks and free up some cash to meet your financial goals. This requires balancing your budget: deciding where you can make cuts and then setting a monthly spending limit for each category of expenses.

Although everyone has different priorities—one woman can't live without her weekly manicure, while another can't live without her kick-boxing class—there are some general guidelines for what you should be spending in categories such as clothing and transportation. The cost of living in your area may also affect these guidelines; in California, for example, housing may eat up 40% of your income.

Category	% of monthly budget
Housing	31
Transportation	18
Food	15
Clothing	7
Entertainment	6
Health care	5
All other	18

Here's how to calculate those percentages: Say you want to budget 15% of your income for transportation, and your take-home pay is $3,000 per month. Multiply $3,000 by 15 and divide by 100. The result is $450 per month. For any other amount you need to calculate, just replace 15 by the percentage you've chosen.

get real!

Setting realistic projections about how much you should save and spend

No matter what your financial situation—even if you are spending well beyond your means and your creditors are banging on the door—it's unrealistic to expect to go from spending $200 per week on groceries to $40. Unfortunately, that's a trap that novice budgeters easily fall into. They expect too much, too soon. When they don't achieve their high goals—and they never do because they're unrealistic—they deep-six the old spending plan and declare all budgets useless.

A better idea? Start slowly and cut expenditures gradually. In fact, the first month of working with your new budget may simply be an adjustment period in which you experiment to see what works and what doesn't.

Perhaps you spent less money this month than you usually do because you had to write it down. Perhaps you forgot to include some expenses due next month. Perhaps you didn't do as thorough

It's about time

You can't budget aimlessly. You need to set a specific time period in which to monitor how you spend and save—be it weekly, bimonthly, or monthly. Monthly budgets are popular because they're so manageable. First you determine how much money you're allowed to spend on, say, groceries. Let's say it's $150 per week. Your monthly grocery budget would then be $600. Over the course of the month, you work with that $600 figure. One week you may spend $175, another $125. It doesn't matter how much you spend per week as long as you keep within that $600 mark for the month.

Weekly budgets, on the other hand, don't provide as much room for that type of give-and-take. Plus, not everyone has the time or the inclination to follow a weekly budget. If you really need to cut costs, though, a weekly plan may give you needed structure.

Some people like to time their budget with their paychecks. If you get paid bimonthly, for example, you might want to have a two-week budget. In addition, some folks also run a yearly budget to make sure that they're on track with their longer-term financial goals. Which time period is best? The one that's easiest for you to stick with.

a job of tracking your expenses as you thought you did. Maybe you created a plan that was too rigid. Often, you just need to live with a budget for a while to know if it's working. Then, you can make adjustments where necessary and make more realistic projections about how much money you should save and spend.

Keep all this in mind as you start putting some numbers into your budget later in this chapter.

ASK THE EXPERTS

I've been trying to stick to my budget, but I always seem to spend money I can't account for. What should I do?

There will always be some money you can't account for. Perhaps it's those new shoes you bought or the Chinese food you picked up on the way home from work last night. We all lose track of our spending on some items. (No one is perfect at sticking to a budget.) But that doesn't mean we can't budget successfully. Call a category "cash" and include these nontracked expenses. Better yet, carry a small notebook and record your cash expenditures so very little ends up in the miscellaneous category.

I created a strict budget and stuck to it religiously—for a week. Then I fell off the wagon and went on a spending spree. What can I do to try to be more disciplined?

Many people kick off their budgeting efforts with a super-strict strategy. None of this. None of that. Not much of anything, in fact. But most of us can't live on just bread and water—not for too long anyway. Within a short time, these spartan budgeters tire of such frugal living and the budget is history. A smarter strategy? Set more modest saving and spending goals at first—goals that leave room to do the things you really enjoy—and gradually increase to more ambitious dollar amounts.

making ends meet

**Trimming costs
without skimping
on necessities**

Even though you've looked at your lists of expenses many times,
you just don't know how you can reduce your spending and still
make ends meet.

You have to cut back. But how? Start by reviewing the expenses you
noted in your spending diary or in the worksheets in Chapter 3.
Look for "luxury" items or services, like housecleaning or mani-
cures, that you can do without—or simply do with less of. Maybe
you truly don't have time to clean, but do you really need a maid
every week? If you can make do with an every-other-week service,
you'll slash that housecleaning expense in half.

Circle any expenses that you think could be trimmed—even by a
small amount. Cut 10 different luxury expenses by a mere $20
each, for example, and you'll save $200 in one month. What's

more, you probably won't even notice those little nips
and tucks.

And don't overlook your fixed expenses. Just because
those costs are fixed doesn't mean that you can't reduce
them. You may be able to refinance your mortgage to
lower your monthly payment, for instance, or find a
cheaper deal on your long-distance phone service (see
Chapter 7). Or you might consider dropping your cable
subscription or switching to a cheaper cell phone plan.

Finally, highlight those expenses you can eliminate
entirely. Could you walk those 10 blocks to the office
every day instead of taking the bus? How about replacing soda with tap water at work and at home? It'll
shrink your expenses—not to mention your waistline!

Snip, snip, snip

Need to spend less? The possibilities are endless. Here are some ideas to get you started:

- Cut down on your dry-cleaning bills by buying only machine-washable clothes.

- Bring rented videos back to the store on time. Those late fees can really add up. Ditto for overdue library books.

- Want to see a movie? Catch the matinee show. It's often cheaper than later show times.

- Take a defensive driving course. In most states, you'll get a discount on your car insurance.

- Stop with the expensive gifts—give of your time instead. Watch your brother's kids for a weekend or give a friend a homemade dinner.

- Cook at home instead of ordering take-out dinners.

- Cancel the premium movie channels on your cable service.

- Cancel the premium services on your home phone. Instead of using voice mail, for example, buy an inexpensive answering machine.

- When looking for a phone number, use the phone book instead of directory assistance.

- Do it yourself—as in, cut your own lawn; polish your nails; paint the house; wash the car—rather than paying someone else to do it for you.

- Cancel some magazine subscriptions. Trade magazines with friends, relatives, and colleagues.

- Buy used books or paperbacks rather than new hardback releases. Or better yet, use your local library or borrow books from friends.

- Eat breakfast at home instead of buying it on the way to work. Make your lunch and take it to work or school.

- Next vacation, camp in the great outdoors instead of staying at a pricey hotel.

savvy splurging

We all need a little "fun" money once in a while

Taking control of your spending is not supposed to be a punishment. It shouldn't mean going without in every aspect of your life—or penny-pinching until there's almost nothing left. Rather, it's more a matter of setting limits. Think of your budget as a gentle guide that will ultimately help you make smarter choices about how you'll use your money.

To stay motivated, don't overdo it. Budgeting efforts that ask you to cut back too much, too fast, generally fail. Why? Most folks quickly tire of such frugal living. You will fare far better if you start slow. Set modest, achievable goals initially, and then gradually increase to more ambitious savings amounts.

Don't forget to make your budget livable. If you love to eat out, for instance, don't completely eliminate that activity just because you're trying to save money. Instead, eat out less often or find restaurants that run specials. Similarly, you don't have to stop taking vacations just because you're following a budget. Perhaps you can scale back—without sacrificing your enjoyment. Travel for one week instead of two, for example, or drive to your destination instead of flying.

Finally, give yourself some breathing room. Set aside a small amount of "fun" money. (That's money you can spend however you choose.) And reward yourself occasionally. Splurging every now and again—especially if you've set aside money for just this purpose—won't derail your spending plan. In fact, this flexibility may actually help you stick with it.

Work it out!

Whether it's a designer handbag or the latest high-tech gadget, we all need to pamper ourselves with the occasional luxury. That's what "fun" money is for. To prevent these purchases from becoming mere impulse buys, however, make a list of those items you'd like to splurge on in the future. (Note the price, availability, and store, catalog, or Internet site where you first saw each thing, then rank each item according to priority.) This way, when you have some extra bucks on hand, you will have a record of what you really wanted—and you won't be as tempted to spend the money impulsively on something you just happen to see.

MY WISH LIST

Item	Availability	Place of Purchase	Cost	Priority

budgeting your debt

Don't count credit card expenses twice

How do you handle debt payments in a budget? Loans that have set monthly payments are easy to figure. With auto and school loans, for example, you pay a predetermined amount each month for a certain number of months (or years). Simply include each payment, then, as a monthly expense—until the loan is paid off. (You should have listed such payments under "Debt" in the Fixed Expenses worksheet in Chapter 3.)

Debts that don't have fixed loan amounts or require set monthly payments, such as credit card balances, are a bit trickier. First, you want to make sure that you're not counting the same expense twice. That is, don't include the cost of that new coat you bought with your Visa card in its specific expense category ("clothing," for exam-

ple) and then also include the credit payments for that coat in your "credit card debt" category. Use one or the other. A smart strategy is to use the "credit card debt" category for balances you've already run up, and put new purchases—even those bought with credit cards— in their specific expense categories.

Second, although credit card balances do require some payment each month, it's a small amount. Making just these minimum monthly payments will not only take a long time to pay off the debt, but also cost you a fortune in interest. (See Chapter 8 for more on credit card debt.) To save money, you need to pay down this debt more aggressively. How? Decide how much you can afford each month, and pencil that amount into your budget next to "credit card debt" payments. No matter how little your minimum payment, this figure is your new monthly payment.

Then work out a repayment schedule that defines how much you need to shell out each month to pay off your debts by a certain date. Actually "seeing" the money wasted on interest payments may spur you to cut back on other expenses temporarily so that you can pay off this debt even faster. Your goal is to eventually delete this "credit card debt" category from your budget.

The real cost of credit card debt

How long would it take you to pay off a $3,000 balance at 12% interest—assuming you didn't incur any more charges? It depends on how much you pay per month. Here's how the numbers add up:

Monthly Payment Amount	Number of Years It Takes to Pay Off Your Balance	Total Interest Paid
$266.55	1	$198.56
$141.22	2	$389.29
$99.64	3	$587.14
$79.00	4	$792.07
$66.73	5	$1,004.00
$58.65	6	$1,222.84
$52.96	7	$1,448.49
$48.76	8	$1,680.82
$45.55	9	$1,919.69
$43.04	10	$2,164.95

FIRST-PERSON DISASTER STORY

Miles to go

For two years I used my credit card for everything—even groceries. I was roped in by a promotion that gave me frequent flier miles for every dollars I charged. Even though I could have paid cash, I kept charging because I was so focused on getting a free ticket to Hawaii. But I didn't check how many frequent flier miles were needed to earn that free trip. It turns out I needed about 30,000 miles, and after two years of out-of-control charging, I had only earned 10,000 miles. And although I had been trying to pay off the balance every month, it had slowly crept up on me until it was over $5,000. Plus, I was paying 20% interest on it! It's going to take me years to get out of this mess. I wish I had read the fine print!

—Lily D., College Grove, TN

budgeting your income

It's time to create your budget

Great! You now have all the basic know-how you need to create your budget. You know what kinds of expenses you can trim, you have a realistic view of what you can accomplish, and you have decided whether you are going to budget on a weekly or monthly basis. Now it's time to use all the calculations you did in Chapter 2 to build your new budget.

Start with your income. On a lined notepad, write the month (or whatever time period you are using for your budget) at the top of the page, along with "Income." You will write up a new page for each time period.

Next, copy the three column headings across the top of the page as they appear at right: "Budgeted Amount," "Actual Amount," and "Difference." Then list the types of income that apply to you and your family. (No brain work is involved here. All you need to do is flip back to the Income worksheet on pages 40–42 in Chapter 2 to find your sources of income.)

Then, under "Budgeted Amount", write in what you think you will earn in each of these categories during the budget period. (Again, you can refer to the worksheets you filled out in Chapter 2 to find the numbers.) As the month goes along, write down the amount of money you actually earned in the second column, "Actual Amount."

At the end of the month, compare the figures in both columns. Does the actual amount equal the budgeted amount? Is it more, or less? The answer belongs in the "Difference" column. Unless your income fluctuates because it is based heavily on a bonus, commission, tips, or freelance work, you probably won't find much discrepancy on the income side of your budget. If your income is consistently coming in under budget, however, then you will have to make some adjustments in the expense worksheets that follow to compensate for the decreased income. Otherwise, you will wind up spending more than you earn.

BUDGET WORKSHEET: INCOME

You worked out the totals for the "Budgeted Amount" column on page 43 in Chapter 2.

Month: _____

	Budgeted Amount	Actual Amount	Difference
Total Salaried Income (includes bonuses, tips, commission, overtime pay, second job, spouse's pay)	_____	_____	_____
Total Self-Employment Income (includes freelance income, royalties, business/partnership income, etc.)	_____	_____	_____
Total Additional Income (includes child support, unemployment benefits, alimony, disability, workers' comp, etc.)	_____	_____	_____
Total Investment Income (includes savings, money markets, stocks, bonds, CDs, mutual funds, etc.)	_____	_____	_____
Total Retirement Income (IRA, 401(k), Keogh, etc.)	_____	_____	_____
Total Other Income (includes an inheritance, cash gifts, rental income, etc.)	_____	_____	_____
Total Monthly Income	_____	_____	_____

budgeting fixed expenses

Fixed expenses typically stay the same every month

The "fixed expenses" part of your budget worksheet gets filled in much like the income pages. On a lined notepad, copy these three column headings across the top of the page: "Budgeted Amount," "Actual Amount," and "Difference." On the left side of the page, write the types of expenses that apply to you and your family using the Fixed Expenses worksheet you filled out on pages 54–55 in Chapter 3.

Then, pencil in what you think you will spend in each category under the "Budgeted Amount" column. Go back to the worksheet you filled out in Chapter 3 to get the numbers.

FIXED EXPENSES

But wait! If you are going to try to cut costs on some of your fixed expenses, then write in the new budget amount here, not the numbers from the worksheet in Chapter 3. For example, if your average utility bill is $150, but you are going to try to reduce it to $125 by setting the thermostat in your house a few degrees lower, then write in $125, not $150, under "Budgeted Amount." (See Chapter 7 for more budget stretchers.)

As the month goes along, pencil in the amount you actually spend during that particular month in the second column, "Actual Amount."

At the end of the month, compare the figures in both columns. Does the actual amount equal the budgeted amount? Is it more, or less? The answer belongs in the "Difference" column.

Typically, as with your income, the difference between the budgeted and actual amount of your fixed expenses won't be great. Your greatest savings are probably going to come from setting new budget limits for variable expenses (see pages 128–129).

BUDGET WORKSHEET: FIXED EXPENSES

You worked these numbers out—in detail—in Chapter 3. (See pages 54–55.)

Month: _____

	Budgeted Amount	Actual Amount	Difference
Housing (rent, mortgage, etc.)	_____	_____	_____
Insurance (auto, health, life, etc.)	_____	_____	_____
Transportation (loan/lease payments, etc.)	_____	_____	_____
Family (tuition, day care, etc.)	_____	_____	_____
Utilities (phone, electricity, heat, etc.)	_____	_____	_____
Debt (credit cards, school loans, etc.)	_____	_____	_____
Savings (IRA, emergency cash fund, etc.)	_____	_____	_____
Total Monthly Fixed Expenses	_____	_____	_____

budgeting variable expenses

Set new, lower numbers here to yield big savings

Here's where the real nitty-gritty of your budget is worked out. Your variable expenses are probably the easiest categories to trim as you create your new budget—and where you will see the most dramatic savings if you stick to your goals.

On your notepad, copy these three column headings: "Budgeted Amount," "Actual Amount," and "Difference. On the left side, list the variable expenses that apply to you. Refer back to the Variable Expenses worksheet you filled out on pages 56–63 in Chapter 3.

Now comes the fun part. Let's say you want to save $200 every month toward your goal of buying a new car within a year. First, review the "Monthly Average" column on your Variable Expense worksheet; these are the amounts you came up with by tracking your expenses for three months. Find the spending leaks—expenses you can nip and tuck to scrape together that $200.

For example, you might decide to cut $100 off your entertainment expenses and $100 off your take-out food expenses. Write the new budget amounts for these expenses in the "Budgeted Amount" column, as shown at right. As the month goes on, track your expenses in your spending diary. Then, at month's end, note how much you really spent in the "Actual Amount" column and calculate the difference. Hopefully, the difference will equal $200—money you should put into a savings account or other savings plan ASAP. (See Chapter 9 for more on savings.) Once you get the hang of budgeting, put this $200 into your savings account as soon as you get paid every month.

A word of warning: Do not expect perfection overnight. It may take a few months to figure out whether you have cut back too much, too little, and in the right places. For example, you may find that although you have stuck to your new budget for take-out food, now you're spending $25 more on groceries. You can work harder to stick to the budgeted grocery amount next month, or you can make up the difference by spending $25 less in another area, such as "holidays and gifts."

Keep it up

Every month, recreate these bugert pages and fill in the amounts as you go along. You can use personal finance software or Excel to create and keep these sheets, too. Keep using your spending diary as necessary to track your expenses, and make adjustments to your budget as you go along. Good luck!

BUDGET WORKSHEET: VARIABLE EXPENSES

You worked these numbers out—in detail—in Chapter 3. (See pages 56–63.)

Month: _____

	Budgeted Amount	Actual Amount	Difference
Housing (repairs, renovations, etc.)	_____	_____	_____
Transportation (gas, maintenance, etc.)	_____	_____	_____
Food	_____	_____	_____
Clothes	_____	_____	_____
Medical and Dental (prescriptions, co-payments, etc.)	_____	_____	_____
Children	_____	_____	_____
Recreation	_____	_____	_____
Personal Care	_____	_____	_____
Pets	_____	_____	_____
Professional Fees	_____	_____	_____
Holidays and Gifts	_____	_____	_____
Miscellaneous	_____	_____	_____
Total Monthly Variable Expenses	_____	_____	_____

now what do I do?
Answers to common questions

I'm working on a monthly budget, but I have expenses like life and auto insurance that I pay once per year. How do I budget for those items?

Since you're working on a monthly budget, take the total amount due and divide it by 12. Let's say, for instance, that your life insurance premium is $500 per year. Divide that $500 by 12 and your monthly payment would be $60. Every month, then, you will have to set aside $60—in a savings or money market account—so that you'll have the money to cover this expense when it arises.

Of course, this works neatly on paper because we're assuming your life insurance is due exactly one year from now. However, in reality, you may have just set up your budget. And your annual insurance premium may come due in 5 months, not 12. This time around (until the budget has been up and running for a while), you will have to set aside more money. Divide the $500 premium by the months you have left until payment is due: in this case, 5. Then, put $100 into your savings account each month. ($500 divided by 5 = $100.) Once you pay that first premium, you can then begin saving on a 12-month cycle.

How long do I need to stay on a budget?

Until you win the lottery. And even then it would still be a good idea. Learning to use a budget is like learning to eat healthy for life, as opposed to crash-dieting once a year to get rid of a few pounds. A budget does require a certain amount of discipline, but with practice, a budget will become easier to maintain, and the benefits should be readily apparent, namely: A good budget will keep you from wasting your money on things that don't matter so you will have more money for things that do.

How often do I need to revise my budget?

As often as necessary, but not more than once per month—or whatever budget time period you're following. In the early stages, you may have to refigure your expenses quite a bit until you get it right. That's normal. Some expenses are more seasonal than others. For example, your electricity bills may be higher in the warmer weather because the air conditioner is on. And other expenses, such as entertainment and holiday gifts, may just be harder to account for. Over time, you will probably need to make more substantial revisions to accommodate major changes in your life, such as the birth of a child, a divorce, or your retirement.

Help! No matter what I do, I can't seem to control my entertainment expenses. What can I do?

That's easy: Don't lump too many expenses—no matter how related they seem—in one catch-all category, "Entertainment." Think about the individual expenses, such as movie tickets, videos, CDs, and magazines. Next month, try breaking down your entertainment category into smaller, separate units, such as music, movies, and parties. It's easier to keep tabs on your spending—especially your discretionary spending—if you track items in very specific categories. Another tip: Try putting your entertainment money in an envelope. When the envelope is empty, you wait until the following month to spend any more on entertainment.

Now where do I go?

Books

Become Totally Debt-Free in Five Years or Less
by Gwendolyn D. Gabriel

Debt-Free by 30: Practical Advice for the Young, Broke, & Upwardly Mobile
by Jason Anthony and Karl Cluck

Debt-Free Living: How to Get Out of Debt and Stay Out
by Larry Burkett

Web Sites

www.bankrate.com
Click on "Calculators," then "Credit Cards," then "What will it take to pay off my balance?" to find out how long it will take to pay off your credit card—and how much interest you'll pay over time.

www.66waystosavemoney.org
The Federal Consumer Information Center and the Consumer Literacy Consortium offer a new edition of *66 Ways to Save Money*, which features tips on how to get better deals on airfares, insurance, cars, and other expenses. Print it out online or request the booklet in the mail by sending 50 cents to:

Save Money, Dept. 60, Pueblo, CO 81009

Budget Stretchers

“*Trimming my expenses was easier than I thought.*”

make each dollar count

Get the most for your money

You've curbed those impulse buys. Set up a livable spending plan. You can track every cent that comes in and goes out. So . . . what's next? If you're committed to enjoying life and living well—but doing so within your means and not with the help of plastic—you need to make every dollar count. It's time to s-t-r-e-t-c-h your imagination (and your wallet) and figure out how you can get the most for your money.

This process will involve some quick (and relatively easy) adjustments to your discretionary spending. It might mean borrowing books from the library instead of buying them at the local bookstore. Switching from incandescent to fluorescent lightbulbs. Hanging your laundry on the clothesline instead of using the electric dryer every day. Using grocery store coupons. Traveling in the middle of the week. Jogging around the park instead of paying for a gym membership.

In many instances, you can stretch your hard-earned dollars simply by being more creative. Trade baby-sitting services with another parent, for example. It won't cost either of you a penny, and you'll both get a free afternoon to attend a yoga class or run errands. Pick up a crafts book or take a craft-making class (adult ed classes at the local high school are generally super-cheap) and make gifts for the folks on your holiday list. Or buy a used piece of furniture and refinish it yourself.

However, these kinds of adjustments can stretch your dollars only so far. To really put some bounce into your budget, you need to play with your fixed expenses, too. That may mean refinancing your home mortgage, lowering your insurance rates, or consolidating your credit card debt with a home equity loan. (Debt is such a powerful factor in the budget equation, in fact, that it's discussed in its own chapter, starting on page 152.)

The bottom line: Whatever you do, make the most of every dollar you spend.

ASK THE EXPERTS

I'm always surprised by the fees charged on ATM withdrawals. How can I reduce them?

Find a bank that has ATMs that are convenient to you and make withdrawals only from them. Otherwise, you'll be charged fees by your bank and the bank or company that owns the ATM machine. If you're stuck, withdraw enough cash so that you don't have to do it again the next day, or you'll be charged the same fees all over again. Say you need only need $20. If you will be charged $5 in ATM fees, you'll pay 25% "interest" on the $20 withdrawal. So if you think you may need more cash later, it makes more sense to withdraw $100 instead, which drops the "interest" you pay to only 5%.

Get your priorities straight

Budget stretching isn't magic, of course. To achieve the financial sleights of hand suggested in the following pages, you will probably have to give up something. While you won't have to sacrifice quality, you may have to relinquish some quantity. Most things in life are trade-offs, and budgeting is no exception. It's a matter of priorities.

The question, then, is: Are you ready to skimp on the things that don't matter too much so that you have money to spend on the things that do? Good. Let's get started.

Five Budget-Stretching Rules to Live By

1. I will shop off-season Prices are low, low, low.

2. I will shop at discount stores, outlet centers, or thrift stores But look for quality merchandise you need. Don't buy something just because it's a bargain.

3. I will think twice before making any purchase How long will I use this item? Am I paying for convenience—or quality?

4. I will buy in bulk Stock up—and save—on necessities.

5. I will recycle Not just soda bottles, but everything I own. Trade kids' hand-me-downs with friends. Use old socks or towels to clean the house or the car.

---

savvy supermarket savings

Shop smarter— and save

Supermarkets are designed to get you to spend money. Ever notice how the cookies, potato chips, and other goodies are stacked where you enter the store—when your urge to buy is at its peak? Or how sale items are typically scattered throughout the store, forcing you to walk through every aisle to get them (and, the managers hope, pick up other, nonsale items along the way)? Understanding these traps—and how to avoid them—will make you a smarter shopper. It'll save you a bundle, too.

One secret to saving while shopping at the supermarket is to confine most of your shopping to the perimeters of the store. This is where you'll find the lower-priced, healthy necessities, such as dairy products, meat, cheese, and produce. Higher-priced packaged goods are almost always found in the center aisles.

Another supermarket layout secret is to beware of the products stacked at the end of every aisle. Not all of them are necessarily on sale. Also, look down when you're shopping: Economy-size and generic items are usually placed on the lower shelves. Smaller, brand-name products—which ring up more profits for the supermarket—are usually set at eye level, the place the shopper looks first.

Shopping dos and don'ts

If you want to shop smart, keep these tips in mind next time you head to the supermarket:

- Don't go shopping on an empty stomach. You're more likely to buy junk food and impulse items—and to spend more than you normally would.

- Consider economy sizes if you have a lot of mouths to feed. Better yet, join a warehouse food club that stocks five-pound jars of jelly, cartons of toilet paper, and cases of soda. When you buy in bulk, the prices are generally much lower.

- Make a list. Buy only what's on the list or what's on sale.

- Watch the prices ring up. Clerks make mistakes—even with those electronic price scanners. The most frequent errors? Sale prices rung up at the regular price because the "new" prices have not yet been entered into the computer.

- Compare unit prices. That's the per-pound or per-ounce price listed on the shelf beneath the product. While larger sizes are generally cheaper, per ounce, than smaller sizes, that's not always true. Sometimes, smaller sizes and individually packaged servings may actually cost less (especially if there's a store special or you have a coupon).

- Don't buy for convenience. You'll pay more for prewashed, precut salad in bags as well as carrots and melons that are already cut up. Generally, the more prepared a food is, the higher its cost.

- Check your local newspaper for grocery specials. Then, plan your meals around these bargains. You'll save money—and be less likely to buy unnecessary products.

- Limit your purchases to groceries. Health and beauty aids, such as toothpaste, shampoo, and hand lotion cost a lot less at a discount drug store.

- Put unplanned extras into the child's seat of the shopping cart. If these impulse buys stay in plain sight, you may reconsider and put them back before getting in line.

- If you are a senior, shop on senior days. Some stores offer discounts on certain days of the week.

clipping coupons

It's well worth the time

Clipping coupons sounds about as cents-ible as hoarding pennies in a piggy bank. A few cents here or there won't make a difference. It's just a waste of time, right? Truth is, you can shave a few dollars (or more) off your weekly supermarket tab by taking advantage of discount coupons. The secret: Make coupons part of your regular shopping routine, without going overboard on the amount of time you spend clipping them.

Some helpful hints include the following:

- **Set a limit.** Coupons turn up everywhere—in newspapers, magazines, unsolicited mail, even the yellow pages. But who has time to do all that clipping? Pick one or two sources—your Sunday newspaper, for example—and then call it quits.

- **Be selective.** Don't be tempted to buy a product just because you have a discount coupon. Instead, collect coupons for products that you normally buy—or for products that you've already decided you would like to try.

- **Comparison shop.** Don't use a coupon without checking out prices of other brands first. An item purchased with a discount coupon may still cost you more than another name brand or generic product.

- **Get organized.** You'll never remember to use coupons if they're stuffed haphazardly into a kitchen drawer. Organize by category—paper goods, cereal, pet food, and so on. If you usually shop in the same store, file according to the layout of the supermarket aisles. Store in an envelope or one of those wallets designed specifically for coupons.

- **Clip in season.** Some coupon-rich seasons? Around the Super Bowl, Easter, Memorial Day, the Fourth of July, and, in anticipation of holiday shopping, the months of October and November.

- **Clip your cash-register receipt.** Many supermarkets now provide electronic coupons. Here's how they work: As the UPC scanner records your laundry soap purchase at the checkout counter,

it also triggers discounts on such future purchases as fabric softener, stain remover, or, perhaps, a rival brand of detergent. These discounts are connected to what you just bought and are printed out on the back of the cash-register tape.

- **Go clipless.** Most supermarkets put out a weekly flyer, advertising specials to its valued shoppers. To get these bargains, customers hand a member card to the cashier, who scans the card into the computer system. Don't have a card? You can generally sign up that day (and still take advantage of the savings). There's no fee for this membership, and you can belong to as many valued shopper clubs as you like.

travel on the cheap

Be budget-smart when traveling

Whether you travel alone, in a group, or with young children in tow, the costs of a vacation can really add up. To be a budget-smart traveler, you're going to have to do more than simply book your stay during the off-peak season. While this common strategy can save you some bucks at certain destinations, it can also backfire. In some vacation spots, rates are slashed during the off-season for a very good reason—because the weather is lousy. What can you do, then, to save money on the road?

Book reservations with the hotel itself Travelers often simply book rooms through a hotel's 800 number, which automatically connects with the hotel's national reservation service—rather than the front desk of the hotel. What's the difference? The 800-number operators quote you prices from their computer screen—and most of the time, those are the highest, nondiscounted prices. Call the hotel directly and ask about weekend rates, seasonal specials, and other discounts, such as those offered to senior citizens. Also, try the hotel's Web site; many have "Web only" specials. When all else fails, simply *ask* for a discount!

Drive instead of fly Obviously, you'll save money on airfare, but you'll also pocket the cash normally spent on a rental car, airport parking fees, and/or taxi fares. If your idea of a vacation doesn't include driving 10 hours to, say, Disney World, then pick a destination that is within an acceptable driving distance. New Yorkers, for example, could drive to Washington, D.C. It's a reasonable drive, and all the government-run museums—including the Air and Space Museum and American History Museum—are free.

Skimp on meals Eating three full meals a day at top restaurants is the fastest way to blow your travel budget. Instead, eat just one meal per day at a fancy eatery. Catch the other two at more modest cafés, or, better yet, opt for a room with a kitchenette and cook breakfast. Another option: Eat lunch (instead of dinner) at the more expensive joints. The menu and portion-sizes may be more modest, but so are prices.

ASK THE  EXPERTS

Can I really save money on by using online travel sites?

Yes, you can, but you have to know where to look and how to shop. There are auction sites and purchase sites. At an auction site (check out sites like **www.priceline.com** or **www.skyauction.com**), you set the amount you are willing to pay for a travel package or flight. If you win the auction, that amount is automatically charged to your credit card and it's nonrefundable, so be sure you know what you're getting into.

You can also try sites such as **www.hotels.com**, **www.travelocity.com**, **www.cheaptickets.com**, and **www.hotwire.com**. On these sites, you can compare prices for hotels and flights, then book what you want. Because these sites often act as travel consolidators, you may be able to get cheaper rates here than if you call a hotel or airline's 800 number.

Fly the friendly skies—for less

- **Travel when other people don't want to** Airfares are priced according to supply and demand. Most folks want to fly between 7:00 and 9:00 a.m. or 4:00 and 7:00 p.m. on weekends, so those flights generally cost more and fill up early. To take advantage of lower fares, travel at the least popular times (that's the middle of the week or late at night), book your trip about three weeks in advance, and plan to stay over on a Saturday.

- **Use your frequent flyer miles** You may not be thrilled that you or your spouse travels a lot on business, but look on the bright side: Some employers will allow you to use all those free miles you earn to travel on vacation with your family.

- **Shop online** Scour the Internet for good travel deals and airline ticket auctions. Sites such as **www.priceline.com** allow you to set your own price for a ticket, and if the company accepts your offer, the ticket will automatically be charged to your credit card. The only drawback is that you often cannot request a specific time and day, but must be somewhat flexible. Also try sites like **www.eBay.com** and check airlines for Internet specials.

- **Take the bump** If you have some flexibility in your vacation schedule, volunteer to give up your seat if your flight is overbooked. Should the airline actually "bump" you to another flight, they will give you a later flight to the same destination—and, as a "thank you" for giving up your seat, a voucher to use toward another round-trip ticket, or (if you're lucky) a ticket that can be used anytime within the coming year.

trimming mortgage payments

Find a mortgage with a lower interest rate

A home owner's monthly mortgage payments generally eat up a good chunk of income. Aside from selling your house and moving to smaller, cheaper quarters, how can you cut costs? Simple. Consider **refinancing** your mortgage—replace your existing mortgage with a new, lower-interest-rate mortgage.

To make this mortgage maneuver worthwhile, however, your new mortgage interest rate should be at least 1% lower than your existing one. Here's why: When you refinance, you need to pay points and closing costs similar to those you paid when you got your original mortgage. The money that you're saving with the lower interest rate should—within a short period of time—make up for these added charges. If it doesn't, then refinancing really won't be saving you any money.

This rule of thumb, however, is just a guide. It doesn't always apply. These days, for instance, you can often get a no-points or no-fee mortgage when you refinance. If that's the case, refinancing may make sense even if you cut your existing rate by as little as half a percent. (See the worksheet on page 143.)

Is the amount of the interest rate the only figure that gets changed when you refinance? Not necessarily. If you like, you can shorten the term of your mortgage: from a 30-year term to a 15-year term, for example. Your mortgage payment may remain the same, but you'll save thousands of dollars over the life of the loan because you won't pay as much interest. You could also replace the type of rate that you have. When refinancing, some folks replace a fixed rate with an adjustable rate (to shrink those payments even more), or an adjustable rate with a fixed rate (to keep those monthly payments more stable over time).

Do the math!

To find out if it's worth it to refinance your home, fill in this worksheet:

	Your Refinancing	**Example**
1. Write your current monthly mortgage payment. (That's principal and interest only. Don't include homeowner's insurance or property taxes.)	_____	$1,500
2. Write your new monthly mortgage payment after refinancing.	_____	$1,350
3. Subtract Line 2 from Line 1. This is the amount you'll save each month by refinancing.	_____	$150
4. Write the amount you'll pay in points and other closing costs.	_____	$3,000
5. Divide the amount on Line 4 by the amount on Line 3. The answer is the number of months it'll take you to recoup the money paid to refinance.	_____	20 Months

If the answer on line 5 is 20 months, for example—and you expect to stay in your current home for more than two years—then refinancing makes sense for you.

reducing utility bills

Save energy— and money

Whether you use oil, natural gas, electricity, and/or other types of fuels, your home energy bills can be a drain on your budget. But you can save money—and be kind to the environment, too—if you take advantage of some of these easy, energy-saving tips:

Turn down the heat You can slash your heating bill by at least 10 percent simply by turning down the heat in your home from 68 to 65 degrees (or even lower) at night. You'll save another 3 to 5% on your hot water heating costs if you lower your water heater's thermostat to 120–125 degrees.

Insulate your water heater Your hot water heater is an energy hog. Did you know it accounts for about 14 percent of the average

household's energy expenses? To lower your costs, wrap your heater in an insulating blanket. This relatively inexpensive insulator can be found at most building supply stores and will pay for itself in just a few months.

Change those bulbs Fluorescent lightbulbs often get a bum rap because they cost more than good old incandescent bulbs. But environmentally friendly fluorescent bulbs use about two-thirds less energy than incandescent bulbs—and they can last up to 10 times longer.

Think layers Most folks know that they should put more insulation—batts, boards, and the sprayed-in foam kind—in the attic, crawl spaces, and exterior walls of their homes to save energy. But did you know that you can insulate outside your home, too? Trees and shrubs planted around your house—especially to the north, east, and west of your home—will cut the wind and keep your house warmer.

Wash your clothes in cold water The hot water cycle uses lots more energy than the cold cycle. And most fabrics wash just as well in a cooler temperature.

Hang a clothesline in the yard Air-drying your clothes instead of using a gas or electric clothes dryer will save you hundreds of dollars a year—and your laundry will get that "spring fresh" scent.

Don't waste water Turn off the faucet while brushing your teeth. Take short showers instead of long, hot baths. (You'll use less hot water.) Install a low-flow showerhead or toilet. It will cut your water consumption in half—without a noticeable difference in pressure. Run the dishwasher only when it's full. (Otherwise, you're wasting hot water—and electricity.) Instead of planting and watering a huge, green lawn—especially in drought-susceptible areas—turn some of your yard into a rock garden or fill some areas with decorative pebbles, wood chips, or cobblestones. Plant hardy cacti, which require less water.

Energy efficient = **cost effective** When buying major appliances like refrigerators and stoves, look for the Energy Star label. This means that the product exceeds the federal government's standards for energy efficiency. When buying a window air conditioner, look for the unit's Energy Efficiency Ratio. For central air systems, look for its Seasonal Energy Efficiency Ratio. In both cases, the higher the number, the more efficient it is.

cutting phone bills

Don't hang up on these substantial ways to save

These days, you can't turn on the radio or open a newspaper without being bombarded with advertisements for discounted long-distance rates. Thanks to continued competition among the various carriers, the savings touted are real. Many folks, though, don't know how to take full advantage of these discounts. The basic tenets below will help you come out ahead in the phone wars.

Rule #1: Get cheaper rates by calling at night and on weekends
Generally, the most expensive time to make a call is during the daytime, so try to make your long-distance calls in the evening and on Saturday and Sunday.

Rule #2: Ask for a discounted calling plan
Don't settle for the standard long-distance rates. They're the most expensive, and they're what the phone companies offer everybody. To find the plan that best suits your needs, you'll have to check with a few carriers. They will be able to find you a cheaper plan by taking into account how many calls you make, when you make them, and which area codes you call.

Rule #3: Consider the perks carefully
When you're comparing plans, rates should be the most important factor. But some carriers try to get your business by offering incentives like frequent flier miles, prepaid calling cards, or even deeper discounts for every dollar you spend on calls. These extras may figure into your final decision, but they shouldn't be the only reason you pick a particular carrier's long-distance plan.

Rule #4: Explore your local calling options
Most carriers offer at least two payment plans for local calls: a flat monthly rate or a per-minute (or per-call) charge. Which is cheaper? For most folks, the flat-rate service wins hands down. But if you don't regularly reach out and touch friends and family over the phone wires—or if you just use the line to send faxes—you might do better with the per-minute option.

Rule #5: Ditch those extra services.

Unless you really feel that you can't live without call waiting, call forwarding, caller ID, three-way calling, and a message center, avoid them. Why? They're expensive: about $50 each per year. (You can pick up an answering machine for $15 at most discount retailers, and it should last for several years.) One last caveat: Don't ever pay for speed dialing. Most phones sold today have this feature built in.

Rule #6: Reevaluate your plan every six months.

You've found the cheapest deal in town—but that could all change tomorrow. Remember that rates change. The competition is constantly trying to under-cut prices, so check twice a year to be sure that you're still paying rock-bottom prices and that the plan still meets your family's phone needs.

FIRST-PERSON DISASTER STORY

A slippery spending slope

When I moved out of my parents' home and got a place of my own, I had to really pinch pennies to make ends meet. I scoured thrift shops for furniture. I clipped grocery store coupons. And I made long-distance calls only at night. I was one smart consumer! But as time went by and I got more promotions and raises at work, I started to drift from those thrifty habits. I didn't have to watch every penny anymore, so I didn't. Not only didn't I watch the pennies, in fact, but I did not watch the dollars, either. Before I knew it, I was making three times the amount that I had earned when I first started out, but I really wasn't any better off. The clincher, I think, was when I couldn't afford to go skiing with a friend one weekend. I had just bought a beautiful leather sofa for $3,000 and I was a little short of cash. The very next day I spotted my sofa at another store on sale for 50% less than I had paid. At that price, I could have had my sofa—and my ski trip, too. I wanted to cry. The lesson? Never give up shopping for discounts and always maintain good spending habits. No matter how much money you earn, you can't afford not to be a smart consumer.

—Jamie W., Allentown, PA

lowering insurance premiums

Cut these costs without sacrificing your safety

At first glance, most kinds of insurance policies seem pretty inexpensive. But as the years pass and your net worth and assets increase, the amount you spend on monthly premiums to insure these assets can start to add up. As part of your budgeting effort, however, you can find ways to reduce your monthly premiums, while not sacrificing basic coverage.

For starters, consider buying all of your policies from the same company, and ask for a multiple-policy discount. You should check the possibility of buying through a group, such as your alumni or business association, because the premiums they receive may be discounted. Finally, ask for a discount if you've stayed with the same carrier for several years.

Also, keep in mind that going through an agent who works only with one insurance provider is often the most expensive route. Instead, consider an independent agent, who may have a wider array of products to suit your needs. Ask for referrals from your lawyer, financial planner, accountant, or friends. Don't work with anyone who pressures you into a policy; select an agent who acts more like an advisor than a salesperson.

Here are more cost-cutting tips that apply to various types of insurance:

Life insurance Many companies, trade groups, and other associations offer life insurance at reasonable prices. Try them before you try the traditional insurance agent. Agents may recommend one company over another because it pays them a higher commission—and not because it's the best buy for you. And look for companies that sell policies directly to the individual; these are called "low-load" or "no-load" policies because they carry no commission. Or go right to the source at sites like **www.insure.com** or **www.quotesmith.com**.

Disability insurance Many companies offer this insurance to their employees. If yours doesn't, then look for a policy with a fixed monthly payment and one that doesn't kick in until at least three to six months after you become disabled. You can also save by turning down special features such as cost-of-living adjustments, residual benefits, and paying a partial benefit if your disability prevents you from working full-time. However, it's probably wisest to simply extend the waiting period instead of cutting these vital benefits.

Home insurance You can reduce these rates by making your home as safe as possible. Do this by installing smoke and carbon-monoxide detectors, fire extinguishers, deadbolt locks, and a security system. Home improvements can help, too; consider upgrading wiring and pipes. And raise your deductible (the amount you agree to pay before the policy kicks in) to as much as you can afford.

Auto insurance If your car isn't worth much more than $1,000, skip the collision coverage and pocket the premium payment. That amount, plus the deductible, would equal what you would get if the car were totaled. Other ways to save include choosing a car that costs less to repair and avoiding cars that insurers hate but thieves love (for a list, see **www.insure.com**). If you receive a ticket or moving violation, contest it or take the suggested actions for removing it from your record (a state-approved defensive-driving class, for example), which will keep your rate low. Also, if your car has safety features such as automatic seat belts or air bags, anti-lock brakes, wheel locks, an ignition cut-off system, or an alarm, request a discount. Finally: Don't smoke! Smokers always pay higher premiums.

Health insurance These days, more and more employers are asking their employees to pay a larger share of their health plans. However, it is usually cheaper than if you have to get individual health insurance. Generally, health insurance is something you do not want to skimp on, but if you do need to purchase your own policy, do some careful research ahead of time. To compare rates, try Quotesmith (**www.quotesmith.com**).

now what do I do?
Answers to common questions

Can I get a cheaper rate on an airline ticket if I'm a senior citizen?

Yes. Almost all airlines give special discounts to travelers over age 62 on virtually all their flights. Just tell the reservation clerk your age when you book your itinerary. They also sell books of coupons that can be used by seniors for trips at reduced prices. Join the American Association of Retired Persons (AARP) and you can save up to 25% on airfare, hotels, motels, resorts, car rentals, and cruises. (To join, you must be over 50; there's a $10 annual membership fee.) As a senior citizen, you can also take advantage of discounts at restaurants, movies, and museums. If you don't see the discounted senior price posted, ask.

I've already done everything I can to lower my energy bills, but they're still astronomical. What should I do?

Call your electricity and/or gas company and ask for a home energy audit. These audits, which are often provided free of charge, are a good starting point to help you identify costly problem areas and figure out how to correct them. They'll look at how well your home is insulated; whether there are weather-stripping gaps in your window and door frames; and whether your heat and cooling systems are working properly and efficiently.

I'm ready to refinance. How can I find the lowest interest rates available?

You could work with a mortgage broker. It's their job to find you the best rates in town—for a fee equal to about 1% or 2% of your loan. But you could also do this research yourself for a lot less money. A good place to start: HSH Associates. Call 1 (800) 873-2837 or visit **www.hsh.com**. The company surveys lenders nationwide about their rates each week and then publishes this information. For about $20, you can buy a report that gives information about the best mortgage deals in your area. You should also try **www.bankrate.com**.

How can I find the good deals in my vacation spot?

Try checking with the visitor's bureau of your destination; they may have a calendar of free seasonal festivals or other special free events, such as Shakespeare in the Park or outdoor bands. Also check the online version of the local newspaper. They may have listings for free days at museums and other specials. Make sure to plan your vacation to include some of these "free" days.

Now where do I go?

Books

Saving Your Way to Success
by Justin P. Ertelt

The Best of the Cheapskate Monthly: Simple Tips for Living Lean in the '90s
by Mary Hunt

The Complete Idiot's Guide to Beating Debt
by Steven D. Strauss and Azriela L. Jaffe

Web Sites

1. Mortgages

■ Apply for a mortgage online at:

www.eloan.com

www.Gomez.com

www.getsmart.com

■ Do your homework! Find out how mortgage rates are this week at:

www.hsh.com

www.bankrate.com

2. Telephone rates

To find out if you're getting the best deal on long-distance phone and cell phone service, check out:

www.LowerMyBills.com

www.MyRatePlan.com

3. Vacation specials

Find great deals—especially at the last minute—on airfare, hotel stays, rental cars, and more at:

www.priceline.com

www.travelocity.com

www.previewtravel.com

4. Everyday savings tips

Get some great cost-cutting advice at:

www.frugaliving.com

Managing Your Debt

CHAPTER 8

"*I finally got my debt under control.*"

too much debt?

If you're losing sleep over bills, then you have too much debt

People fall deep into debt for many different reasons. Some can't live within their means. That forces them to live from paycheck to paycheck—and, often, to rely upon credit cards to stretch their buying power. Others borrow too much for housing. That doesn't leave them any extra cash to pay down existing debt, create an emergency fund, or save for upcoming expenses like a new car or college tuition.

How much debt, though, is actually bad for you? Financial experts offer a variety of guidelines. Some say that taking on any debt—other than for a home or a college education—is bad news, whereas others think it's perfectly acceptable to go into debt for a car or furniture as long as you don't go overboard. While there is no magic debt number, most financial experts agree that your total debt payments should be 25% or less than your take-home pay each month.

No matter how those numbers look on paper, however, if that stack of bills is stressing you out, then you have too much debt. It's that simple. And this is where the budget you've created can help; you can use the money you save by cutting expenses to start paying down that debt, giving yourself extra breathing room.

Credit-card crash landing

Some warning signs that you're in over your head with your credit cards:

- You don't know how much money you owe.

- You make just the minimum payments on your credit card bills each month.

- You regularly miss a monthly payment or make late payments.

- You always use your credit card to buy groceries and other essentials. (You used to pay cash for these items.)

- You sometimes have to choose which bills to pay.

- Occasionally, you use cash advances from your credit card to pay other bills.

using credit cards wisely

Use your credit cards for an emergency only

HOT TIP

If you are having trouble getting a major credit card, try getting a department store card. Though they have outrageous interest rates, these are often easier to get and can help you build a good credit history. Just pay off that balance every month!

A credit card is mighty convenient. It's easier to carry around than cash. It provides monthly records of how much you spent and what you bought. And it can be converted to emergency cash when your ordinary budget plans go awry. The trouble is, a credit card also makes it ever so easy to spend money you don't have. Since no cash actually changes hands when you purchase an item with a credit card, it almost feels like you're not really paying for that item. You can be fooled into quickly spending beyond your means.

It doesn't have to be that way, though. Take control of your credit cards and you can reap all of the rewards—and none of the risks. One of the rewards is the "grace period": If you pay your balance every month, no interest is charged, and you may get to delay paying for an item for several weeks. Using credit wisely will also help you build good credit so you can borrow to buy a home some day. You may also earn flight miles.

Credit card issuers want your business—especially if you pay your bills on time and have an established credit history. That means you can afford to be choosy when it comes to picking a credit card. Look for cards with:

No annual fees Most cards don't charge annual fees anymore. If your card does, call the issuer and ask if they'll waive the fee. If not, find another card.

Low interest rates If you tend to carry a balance on your card from month to month, you really need one of these lower-rate cards. Find out how long the low rate will last. Some issuers offer a teaser rate for six months; then the low rate expires and you're stuck with a much higher rate. At that point, you could always switch to another low-rate card. (The practice is known as credit surfing. It's perfectly legal to do, though excessive surfing can damage your credit. And find out if there's a fee for transferring your balance.) Also, check if the low rate applies to just the balance transferred or to new purchases as well.

Credit rules to live by

Pay off your balances each month It doesn't matter how many purchases per month you make with your credit card. Just be sure to pay those balances off in full. If you can't pay off the entire debt when the bill arrives, plan to pay it off in no more than three payments. Otherwise, put off the purchase until you've stockpiled some cash.

Don't spend just to earn rewards Charging all kinds of stuff you don't need to gain additional points is just plain foolish. You'd fare better if you simply bought your own airline tickets (or whatever freebies the card is offering). Rewards cards typically carry a higher interest rate than other cards and may charge an annual fee, so be sure to pay your balance in full each month.

Only take out a cash advance if it's absolutely necessary If you need money in a hurry, taking a cash advance against your credit card is probably one of the quickest ways to get it. But it's also one of the most expensive forms of borrowing. Interest rates are often higher for cash advances than for regular purchases. And many issuers charge an additional "cash advance" fee. What's more, there is generally no grace period. Unlike purchases, cash advances accrue interest charges immediately.

Keep things simple Limit yourself to just one or two major cards, such as a Visa, a Mastercard, or an American Express. Do you really need all those others? Pay them off, close the accounts, and cut up the cards.

understanding your credit card

Know your credit card terms

Most folks carry a walletful of credit cards and say "charge it" faster than the dollar signs can ring up on the cash register. But few people read the fine print—as in, the cardholder agreement—that accompanies these potent pieces of plastic. The following are common terms you're likely to see on your credit card bill. Read them carefully. Misunderstanding them can cost you a bundle.

Interest rate When you borrow money, you pay a certain percentage on top of the loan for the privilege of borrowing it. That's called interest. With a credit card, your interest rate (also known as a finance charge) is the amount you're charged on the debt if you don't pay off your balance in full. Rates can vary from a low 4.5% to 22% or higher. Credit cards also charge compound interest. That means you pay interest on your initial purchase as well as any subsequent interest if you don't pay off the purchase right away. And remember: credit card interest is not tax deductible, which makes this type of debt very expensive.

Annual fee This is the amount some companies charge you just to keep your credit card account active for one full year. Even if you did not make a single purchase during the year, you'd still have to pay this fee. It ranges from $20 to about $75. If you pay your credit card balance in full each month, it doesn't make sense to use a card that carries an annual fee. Thanks to increased competition among borrowers, most banks don't charge annual fees anymore.

Grace period This is the number of days you have until you're charged interest on your purchases. The usual grace period is at least 25 days. If you carry a balance from one month to the next, however, you generally forfeit your grace period: New purchases are hit with finance charges immediately. The only time you get a grace period, then, is when the previous balance on your statement was zero or you paid last month's balance in full.

Minimum payments Every month, your credit card bill lists a minimum payment due. No matter how much money you actually owe, all you must pay this month is that amount. Typically, this minimum payment is based on a percentage of your total balance due. Sounds like a good deal, right? As long as you're making those minimum payments, you've got those bills under control? Wrong. Lower minimum payments just keep you in debt longer. If you make just the minimum payment each month, a balance of $2,500 (with an interest rate of 18%) will take more than 30 years to pay off. And it'll cost more than $6,500 in interest. Wow.

Penalty fees Paid less than the minimum amount due? Missed the due date? Went over your credit limit? You could be slapped with a penalty fee of up to $35. Some issuers actually raise your interest rate if you make late payments or if your credit rating drops due to nonpayment or late payment of other debts.

RED FLAG

Credit card issuers are permitted to change interest rates, add late payment charges, and even shorten grace periods as they see fit. They must send you a new agreement outlining these changes, of course, so make sure you review this information when you receive it.

kicking the credit habit

Pay off credit cards with the highest interest rates first

Your credit card debt may seem insurmountable—and you're not alone. As Americans, we charge everything from back-to-school clothes to family vacations to holiday gifts. The majority of us are maxed out on our credit cards and can barely make the minimum payments each month. If you are serious about getting rid of your credit card debt, here are the first, most basic steps to take:

Stop charging everything Obvious advice? Yes, but for super spenders this may be the toughest assignment. No matter how Herculean your efforts to pay down existing debt, you won't come out ahead until you stop piling up additional debts and finance charges. Whenever possible, make purchases with cash.

Keep only one card for emergencies You don't need more than that. Try not to use it for impulse purchases. If you slip up, make sure to pay for the item when it appears on your bill to avoid adding to your balance.

Make your other cards inaccessible You'll be less tempted to use them if they're not within easy reach. Put your cards in a safe deposit box, or try this trick: Freeze them in a sealed plastic bag of water! (Quickly thawing them in the microwave doesn't work; the cards melt.) Why not just cancel them? That's always an option, of course. But if you don't have an emergency fund, you'll want to keep your access to available credit open, just in case you need it.

Shift balances to a low-rate card Get the lowest-interest-rate card that you qualify for. (See page 156 for details.) That will keep your interest payments down.

Set modest—and realistic—repayment goals Don't just say you want to pay down your balances. That's too broad (and it'll take too long). You're apt to get discouraged and retreat to your old spending patterns. Instead, set an achievable goal, such as paying off one specific card or a certain amount of your balance. To keep the momentum going, write your goal down and post it where you can see it. Once you reach your goal, do something special. (Nothing that costs much money, of course.)

Make more than the minimum monthly payment This is the only way to win this high-interest game. Start with the card that has the highest interest rate—not the biggest balance.

tap into other resources

Use any extra cash to pay down debt

Paying off outstanding credit card debt as quickly as possible is your goal. If you have cash stockpiled in a savings account, you should use those funds to pay off your credit card debt. Why? Because the interest you are earning on your savings is less than the interest the credit card company is charging you. You may have other untapped sources of income that can help lighten your debt load, too. Here are some ideas:

Ask to trade vacation days for cash Some companies will let you trade a week or two of vacation for the equivalent salary.

Call in money owed to you This is the time to ask your brother to repay you for the loan you gave him for that trip to Europe.

Sell unwanted stuff Haven't used those cross-country skis in ages? Ditto with the camping equipment and that tract of land upstate? If you have an asset or property that you or your family does not use, think about selling it to pay off debt. You'll pocket even more money if the item required costly upkeep or maintenance, such as docking space for a boat. Hold a garage sale to get rid of smaller items collecting dust in the attic, or try selling them on eBay (**www.eBay.com**). You might be surprised at how much you can make.

Increase your income to pay down debt If you're eligible for a bonus or a raise, direct those funds straight to your debt pile. Don't use them to simply increase your standard of living. Consider taking a second job, working overtime, doing freelance work, or asking a family member (i.e., your teenage son or a stay-at-home spouse) to get a part-time job to help with family expenses, which will free up funds to put toward your debt.

Check your credit report

If you've missed a few payments or simply want to see how you rate as a borrower, check out your credit report. This is a public record of your history of paying your debts. Your credit information is gathered by companies called credit bureaus that sell it to anyone with a legitimate interest in giving you credit: for example, a bank that is considering your loan application. What's in the report? A list of how much money you've borrowed and from which institution; whether you made payments on time or ever missed a payment; whether you've ever filed for bankruptcy; whether you ever had a credit lien (a creditor's claim against your property); and whether you have been sued successfully.

Based on this information, you're given a **credit rating**, which is assigned to you based on the amount of money you have borrowed in the past and how you repaid it. A credit bureau sells a copy of your credit report to any institution, such as a bank, credit card company, or mortgage company, whenever you apply for a loan. (Sometimes they give it to prospective employers, too.) If your credit rating is good, you will get the most favorable rates available. If not, then fixing your credit report should become your top priority.

To get a copy of your credit report, write to these three major credit bureaus. Usually you must pay a small fee, unless you have recently been turned down for credit. Even if you haven't been turned down, you should check your credit reports at least once a year, especially given the rise in identity theft. And don't just check one of them—often the three credit reports have different information, so review them all for discrepancies.

Experian	**Equifax Credit**	**TransUnion LLC**
Tel: 1 (888) 397-3742	**Information**	**Consumer**
www.experian.com	**Services, Inc.**	**Disclosure Center**
	P.O. Box 740241	P.O. Box 1000
	Atlanta, GA 30374	Chester, PA 19022
	Tel: 1 (800) 685-1111	Tel: 1 (800) 888-4213
	www.equifax.com	**www.transunion.com**

borrowing to pay debts

It sounds crazy, but borrowing to pay off debts often makes sense

Going deeper into debt may seem like the last thing you'd want to do. But taking out a loan to pay down credit card debt may make sense. Why? Often, you can borrow money at a less expensive interest rate than you are currently paying to the credit card company. It will also simplify your bill paying, and if you're being nagged by collection agencies, it will get them off your back. One of the most popular borrowing options for this purpose is what's called a **debt consolidation loan**.

Here's how it works: A bank agrees to loan you a lump sum of money, which you use to pay off all your credit card debt. You then

pay back the loan (with interest) in agreed-upon monthly installments. You'll save money if the interest rate that the bank is charging is lower than the various rates you're now paying on your credit cards. You'll also save money if you get a loan with a fixed interest rate rather than an adjustable one.

To consolidate your debts, you can take out a personal loan from your bank. (The bank will typically ask for collateral—that's an asset, such as your home or a car—to back up the loan.)

Another option is to borrow against the equity in your house by taking out a **second mortgage** or an **equity line of credit**. A second mortgage works much like a first mortgage. You borrow a fixed amount of money, which you receive in a lump sum, using your home as collateral. An equity line of credit, on the other hand, works more like a credit card. Upon approval, you're granted a maximum credit line that you can draw on (in full or in part) over a certain period of time. Both of these home equity options give you extra cash and let you pay it back at a rate lower than most consumer loans. In addition, the interest paid on these types of loans is tax deductible. The interest paid on credit card debt is not.

Borrow against your assets

If you own a home, you can borrow against the equity built up in the house. But you also may have other assets on hand from which to borrow money.

Your Retirement Plan Many 401(k) plans let you borrow money from your account. By law, you can borrow up to 50 percent of your account's vested assets, or $50,000, whichever is less. No taxes or early-withdrawal penalties are incurred with such a loan—no matter what your age—unless you don't pay the money back. The benefits of such a loan? You pay the money back, with interest, to your own account. The interest rate is generally low, and you can get the money quickly. (Since you're essentially borrowing your own money, no credit check is required.) There are some drawbacks, however. First, over the long term, you're depleting your retirement savings. And, second, you may have to repay the loan immediately if you get laid off or change jobs. Whatever you do, don't "cash out" your retirement savings plan to pay off credit card debt. The tax and penalty for doing so is too high. Take out a loan against the plan instead, if possible. (You cannot do this with IRAs, however.)

Your Life Insurance Policy You can borrow against the cash value of your whole or variable life insurance policy—and never pay it back. You won't be hit with a penalty, either. The amount that you borrow is simply deducted from the death benefit paid to your beneficiaries when you die. As enticing as that sounds (especially if you're faced with a mountain of debt), remember that life insurance is bought as protection for your family. If you deplete the amount to be paid at your death by borrowing against the funds now, you're defeating the purpose of buying the insurance in the first place. (Term insurance does not have any cash value, so you cannot borrow against it.)

dealing with creditors

The best approach is honesty—with yourself and your creditors

If you can't make even the minimum payments on your credit card bills, you may be tempted to stop opening your mail—or to unplug the phone. But hiding from your credit card troubles won't make them disappear. Getting your finances in order means not only working with a budget, but also facing your creditors, if necessary, to work out a repayment schedule.

Many people who aren't able to pay their bills don't tell their creditors. They simply ignore their bills, month after month. (That's exactly what you should *not* do.) Finally, the creditor sends the account into collection, and the bill collector comes knocking at the door. If you can't pay a bill, contact the creditor directly and explain the problem. Say, for example: "I lost my job in July and I'm having some difficulty meeting my payments." Explain how much cash you currently have available to pay your bills, how many other creditors you have, and how much money you owe them.

What good will this do? Lenders hate bankruptcy (it means they probably won't get repaid at all), so they're often happy to work with you to arrange some sort of repayment plan. If you're unable to make the full payment, tell them you'll make at least a partial payment (if this is possible for you) until you're in a stronger financial position. Some creditors may be willing to renegotiate the amount that you owe.

When speaking to creditors, make sure that you note the names of the people you speak with—and what they tell you to do. Once you hit upon a repayment agreement, get it in writing.

ASK THE  EXPERTS

I recently purchased a copy of my credit report and there are several errors in it. What can I do?

If your credit report needs fixing, you are not alone. About 70% of consumers in the United States have at least one negative, wrong item in their credit reports. If you can explain the problem—say, a missed credit card payment due to a hospital stay—you can write down your explanation in 100 words or less and submit copies of it to the three major credit bureaus, and they will attach it to your file. Bad items, such as filing for bankruptcy, stay on your report for 10 years.

FIRST-PERSON DISASTER STORY

Credit card catch-up

I knew I was in trouble, but I just didn't know how much. Business had been kind of slow, and since I work on commission, I was feeling a bit strapped for cash. One month, finally, I just couldn't make all of my payments. So I threw my two credit card bills in the trash. They'll catch up with me next month, I said to myself. Well, business didn't pick up much, and one month turned into six. Before you know it, the girl at the checkout said I couldn't use my card. "It's been denied, sir," she said. I was mortified. Not to mention without a gift for my best friend's birthday. The next morning I got a call about my late payments from some collection agency. They called me every morning for three weeks. I didn't know what to do. They wanted money—and I didn't have it. I tried to call the credit card companies to explain, but once a debt goes to collection, it's out of their hands. Unfortunately, I had to borrow money from my brother to pay the collection agency. Now I'm in debt to him and I have a black mark on my credit record. I wish I hadn't ignored those bills!

—Austin M., Richfield, ID

debt counselors

**It may be
time to seek
professional help**

You've tried cutting your expenses, talking to your creditors, even moonlighting at a weekend job. But it's not working. You're still up to your eyeballs in debt. Not to worry. It may simply be time to seek outside help from a debt counseling service.

The best organization to help you manage your debt is probably the Consumer Credit Counseling Service (**www.cccs.org**). This non-profit group offers free (or very low-cost) debt counseling over the phone and in person. What will a counselor do for you exactly? First, he or she will ask you detailed questions about your family's living expenses and debt. From that information, the counselor will create a workable budget and repayment plan. Then, if necessary, the counselor will contact each of your creditors to arrange a new payment schedule. (Typically, this schedule involves smaller payments made over a longer period of time.) Finally, your debt counselor will teach you how to keep track of expenses, stop impulse spending, and change your attitude about money.

You'll make one monthly payment to the service, out of which they will pay your creditors. Be advised, however, that you will be put on a tight leash until you're in the red again; these payments will be made on a fairly aggressive schedule. Your creditors will get much of your incoming cash, while you are allowed to keep only a small allowance for essential living expenses. If this seems too overwhelming, ask the counselor if he or she can arrange a more lenient payment schedule.

ASK THE  EXPERTS

These debt counseling services will help me manage my debt. But are there any programs that will help me fix the real problem: my overspending?

Yes. Debtors Anonymous, a national not-for-profit collective, offers free referrals and advice for chronic overspenders. You'll find others working to beat the same problem. Contact this group at:

P.O. Box 920888
Needham, MA 02492
Tel: 1 (781) 453-2743
www.debtorsanonymous.org

A debt consolidator called me and said he can fix my bad credit rating. Is this true?

No, unfortunately. Debt consolidators may claim they can clean up a credit report, but it is just not true. Only you can clean it up, and it takes time and effort. You have to contact each creditor and work out a payment plan. Some creditors may agree to lower your interest rate for this purpose, because their main goal is to get paid. Once your debts have been paid off, you can ask your creditors to report your clean slate to the credit bureaus (see page 163), so your credit history shows your improved status.

RED FLAG

Don't confuse respectable, nonprofit debt counselors with those credit repair clinics (or debt doctors) that advertise on late-night TV. For a few hundred dollars, these slick operators promise to magically clean up your credit—or even get you more credit! Only you can clean up your debt problems, and it's not by using magic. These debt doctors don't do anything that you can't do on your own, for free.

bankruptcy

Know what to expect before you file

An individual going bankrupt isn't as unusual as it used to be. Personal bankruptcies have, in fact, skyrocketed over the past two and a half decades—thanks, in part, to aggressive credit card marketing and consumers' eagerness to buy on credit. Although filing for bankruptcy—a federal proceeding that freezes your payment obligations while you work out a repayment schedule with your creditors or petition a court to cancel your debt—basically ruins your credit rating for 10 years, it can provide the fresh start that some people need. And, while it certainly isn't a quick-fix scheme or even an alternative to overspending, bankruptcy may be your best (and only) option when all other efforts to regain your financial footing have failed.

Individuals may file for one of these two types of bankruptcy:

Chapter 7 This "straight" bankruptcy filing wipes out most debts. Your assets (such as a car, a house, or a boat) are auctioned off and the cash is distributed among your creditors. Most remaining debts are canceled. For individuals, this is the most severe form of bankruptcy because it means selling nearly all of your assets. Which assets can you keep? That depends on the state you live in. Most states let you keep personal belongings, such as your furniture and wedding ring. Others may even let you keep your car or home.

Chapter 13 Formerly known as the "wage earners plan," this type of bankruptcy is for people with steady incomes who could pay off their debts if they had more time. A Chapter 13 doesn't wipe out your debt: it reorganizes it. Under this arrangement, you don't sell your assets. Instead, you pay back your debts on a two- to five-year schedule arranged by a court-appointed trustee. You send the trustee a monthly check, and he pays your creditors. Typically, creditors look more kindly upon Chapter 13 bankruptcy than Chapter 7, so it will be easier to reestablish credit in the future.

ASK THE  EXPERTS

Bankruptcy is such a serious step. How do I know if I should consider it?

Here's a rule of thumb that credit counselors use: If your total debt is more than double your annual income (and if you don't expect a raise anytime soon), bankruptcy may be the best course of action to restore your financial security.

Will all of my debts be canceled if I declare bankruptcy?

No. Even if you file for bankruptcy, you're still required to pay most taxes and make student-loan, child-support, and/or alimony payments.

Will bankruptcy permanently destroy my credit rating?

No. You won't be able to borrow any money for about six years. And your bankruptcy filing will stay on your credit report for 10 years, then it will be removed from your file. After this time, however, lenders are still permitted to ask if you've ever declared bankruptcy (and why). This is most likely to occur if you're applying for a big loan.

Do I need a lawyer to file for bankruptcy?

You're not required to have an attorney—but you'll probably want one. Bankruptcy filings are complex, and the ramifications will last for years. A good bankruptcy lawyer can guide you through this quagmire. For a reference in your area, contact your local bar association or the American Board of Certification, which certifies bankruptcy lawyers. Visit **www.abcworld.org** or call 1 (703) 739-1023.

now what do I do?

Answers to common questions

Isn't a debit card just like a credit card?

Not exactly. A debit card often looks like a credit card and is just as convenient. But you're not getting credit—the money is immediately subtracted from your checking or savings account. So there are no bills—and no finance fees—to pay at the end of the month. There are drawbacks, however, to using nothing but a debit card: You don't build a credit rating with it. Also, some cards charge usage fees ranging from 50 cents to $1 per purchase. Finally, if you are renting a car, the car rental company may not accept a debit card.

If my credit card debt is so bad, why do companies keep offering me more credit cards?

Credit card companies have more liberal lending guidelines than banks or other credit institutions. Credit card companies calculate that you can carry debt equal to 36% of your annual gross income, while debt counselors suggest no more than 20%. Credit card companies want you to run up bills because they make their profits from all that interest you're paying. So the more you charge, the more your mailbox seems to fill up with offers for yet more credit cards from companies eager to take advantage of your penchant for spending.

What happens if I don't pay my minimum payment?

That's not a good idea. As far as the credit card company is concerned, that minimum payment is a loan payment. If you miss the deadline, they report it to the credit bureaus that keep track of your credit rating, and it is recorded on your credit report as a missed payment. This can hurt your credit rating.

What if a creditor is harassing me?

That is against the law. Bill collectors are not allowed to use threats, advertise your debt to the public, or phone you repeatedly about it. If one does, contact the Federal Trade Commission (FTC). It monitors and investigates complaints about consumer credit practices.

Federal Trade Commission
600 Pennsylvania Ave., NW
Washington, DC 20580
Tel: 1 (877) 382-4357
www.consumer.gov or **www.ftc.gov**

Now where do I go?

Books

Smart Money: How to Be Your Own Financial Manager
by Ken and Daria Dolon
Written by husband-and-wife financial planners, this covers personal finance basics in a question-and-answer format.

Lew Altfest Answers Almost All Your Questions About Money
by Lewis J. and Karen C. Altfest
Another comprehensive personal finance book written by a husband-and-wife team.

Web Sites

www.bankrate.com
www.bestrate.com
Two financial Web sites that make it easy to find credit cards with competitive interest rates.

www.cccs.org
The Consumer Credit Counseling Service
1 (800) 923-CCCS

www.nfcc.org
The National Foundation for Credit Counseling
1 (800) 388-2227

www.MyVesta.org
A nonprofit consumer education organization.

www.law.cornell.edu/topics/bankruptcy
www.swiggartagin.com/bkfaq
Two sites for learning more about bankruptcy.

Making the Most of Savings

CHAPTER 9

"*My investments are really starting to pay off.*"

savings basics

Knowing how to save is an important part of budgeting

TIP

Write down your savings goal—and post it in a prominent place. Or if you're saving to buy a home, put a picture of your dream house on the refrigerator or next to your computer screen. Visual reminders can help make your goals seem more real.

You've been sticking to your budget for a while now. You're easing your debt burden and starting to break even. Or, even better, you're out of the financial woods and starting to see a little extra money at the end of the month. Well done! This is why you set up a budget in the first place—to break the cycle of spending and to start saving toward your goals. You can boost your savings potential even more using these time-tested tactics:

Put money toward your savings before anything else In other words, pay yourself first. This advice, spouted by every financial guru worth his or her weight in above-average market yields, still reigns supreme. Think of your monthly savings commitment as a fixed expense that must come out of your paycheck immediately, just like your rent or mortgage payment.

Don't keep increasing your standard of living Most people live up to their income. That is, their expenses rise to their level of income—no matter how high their income is. A smarter savings strategy: Next time you get a raise or a promotion, pretend that you didn't. Bank those extra bucks instead.

Once you have started saving, stick with it Even when unexpected expenses crop up, don't raid your savings account to pay for them. Figure out another way to pay for those new expenses.

Start saving as soon as you can Here's why: Your money grows through a process called compounding. That is, you earn interest on your original investment and, over time, you even earn interest on your interest. The key to compounding is time. If you put your money in a secure investment, the longer you let your investment compound, the larger your savings can grow. That's why starting to save early can make such a big difference.

But it's just a cup of coffee!

You work hard for your money. The least you can do is reward yourself with a stop at your local coffee bar on the way to the office, right? Besides, it's only a few bucks. How much damage can that really do?

Unfortunately, plenty. Those little expenses may surprise you by how fast they add up. Take that little cup of joe, for example. A cup can run you about $2.50. You drink a cup each morning, so you'll spend $12.50 on coffee each week. In one year (assuming you take two weeks for vacation), you will spend $625 on coffee. And that's just for the morning. If you take a coffee break in the afternoon, too, you can double that figure to $1,250.

Invest that same $1,250 in a mutual fund earning 8% annually instead (see page 192), and you'll double your money in eight years. In 16 years, you'll have $5,000; in 24 years, you'll have $10,000. All that for giving up your coffee fix for one year! Think of the money you'd save if you gave up that mid-afternoon candy bar, the newest shade of nail polish, and those little "somethings" that you're always picking up for the kids. You might reach your financial goals—ahead of schedule.

savings options

What you need to consider as you choose your savings strategy

Setting aside some money is the first part of the savings equation. Then you have to figure out where to put it. You could stash it in a savings account. If you're saving for a short-term goal, such as stockpiling extra money to pay off a credit card, this may be a good option. But the interest rate on a passbook savings account is minimal, so this type of account is definitely not the place for money that you hope will grow into a nest egg over time.

If you really are serious about building that nest egg, you'll need to consider these factors before you decide where to put your hard-earned cash:

Investment return How much money your investment will earn over time is called its return. While an investment's past performance is no guarantee of future performance, historical data can often be used to help you estimate future returns.

Taxes The government will slap what's called a capital gains tax on the profits and dividends your investments earn. However, retirement accounts are generally tax-deferred. That is, you aren't taxed on the money earned on your investments until you withdraw the money at retirement.

Inflation Historically, prices go up approximately 3% a year due to **inflation**. That's why you never want to resort to the age-old mattress-stuffing method of saving; every dollar you hide away today will buy only 97 cents of goods next year. Or look at it this way: $1,000 put under the mattress today will be worth $859 in five years or $737 in 10 years. Ouch! But there is a remedy: Invest your money so that it earns a rate of return that is higher than inflation.

The magic of interest

One of the magical things about saving money is that the more you save, the more it grows. This is because of interest, or a percentage you earn for putting your savings in certain investments. Another magical thing about interest: The interest you earn on the principal (the money you save) is also earning interest. This is called compound interest.

Compound interest can make all the difference when it comes to achieving your financial goals. To give you an idea: $10,000 invested at 8% for 10 years will have a different yield (the money you get from interest), depending on whether the interest is compounded daily, weekly, quarterly, or annually. You will have $21,589 at the end of 10 years if it's compounded annually, and $22,253 if it's compounded daily—a difference of $664.

Whatever your financial goals are—getting a college education, buying a house—if you start to harness the power of compound interest, you will be able to reach them much sooner.

The rule of 72

Want to know how fast your savings will grow? Use the "rule of 72." Divide 72 by the interest rate on your account. The answer is the number of years it will take for your money to double. For example: Let's say that you put $10,000 into a mutual fund. The account earns an interest rate of 9%. In eight years (72 divided by 9 = 8), you'll have $20,000—or double the original amount.

tax-deferred savings plans

Protecting your stash from taxes

It's one of the common complaints of people who are committed to saving money: "I work so hard to put this money aside, and then the government takes a big chunk of it in taxes every year!" It's true that the earnings on most investments are taxed each year. However, you can stretch your savings by putting some of your money into a tax-deferred savings plan. Traditionally, people use these as retirement funds. And starting a retirement fund should be one of your primary savings goals.

These are the tax-deferred plans you can choose from:

Traditional IRA Short for Individual Retirement Account, this allows you to invest up to $3,000 a year ($3,500 if you are 50 or older) in basically any kind of fund you want. Best of all, you don't have to pay taxes on what you squirrel away until you withdraw it after age 59½. Not only that, but you may be able to deduct that $3,000 from your gross income every year, which reduces your total income tax. However, you can't get the initial tax deduction if you are single and earn more than $50,000 or if you are married and earn more than $70,000. You also cannot get the deduction if you or your spouse participates in a qualified plan at work.

Roth IRA This type of IRA is for single people who make less than $95,000 or married people who make less than $150,000. Unlike a traditional IRA, a Roth IRA does not offer an annual tax deduction. However, when you withdraw the money after age 59½, all the earnings are tax free. (See page 103 for information on the Coverdell Education Savings Account, which is similar to a Roth IRA but can only be used to pay for college.)

SEP IRA This "Simplified Employee Pension" is a savings plan for self-employed people. You are allowed to put up to 20% of your business's annual pretax net earnings, or up to $200,000, in a SEP IRA. As with other IRAs, the taxes on money invested in a SEP IRA are deferred until you withdraw your earnings after age 59½.

401(k) This savings plan, sponsored by employers for their employees, allows you to invest pretax dollars in a selection of mutual funds chosen by the company. The employer selects the mutual funds, but the employee decides how much to put into each one. And to sweeten the pot, some companies contribute an amount equal to what an employee sets aside in a 401(k) account. This is known as "corporate matching." Again, any money saved in a 401(k) is tax-deferred until it's withdrawn at retirement—usually at age 65.

ASK THE  EXPERTS

What kind of taxes will I have to pay on my investments?

It depends on what kinds of investments you have, how much you earn on them, and how long you have them. For example, if you sell stocks, bonds, or shares in a mutual fund for more than you paid for them, you will have to pay what's called capital gains taxes. If this gain happened within one year, or short term, it will be considered regular income and will be taxed at whatever income tax rate you qualify for—probably 25% to 35%. However, if you hold an investment for at least one year before selling it at a profit, this is called a long-term gain, and you will be taxed at either 5% or 15%, depending on your total income. Additionally, any interest you earn will be taxed at your regular rate. And generally you will have to pay state tax on capital gains, dividends, and interest, too. On the other hand, if you sell your investments for less than what you paid for them, this is called a capital loss, and you can deduct up to $3,000 of that loss from your income taxes. Obviously, taxes can play a major role in how much you earn overall from your investments, so smart investors consider the tax consequences before they invest.

money markets and more

Other safe savings options

Your first savings nest egg should go into an investment that is as secure as possible. You certainly don't want to lose that initial pile of savings due to stock market fluctuations! In addition to the tax-deferred savings plans described on page 180, there are several secure investments you should consider. After that first lump of cash is safely tucked away and earning interest, you can think about making riskier investments.

You can learn more about the investing plans described below by visiting your bank or a credit union that has FDIC insurance.

Certificate of Deposit (CD) In this type of investment, you deposit your money in the bank, which pays you a set interest rate for a certain period of time. This is usually one, two, three, or six months—or one, two, three, or five years. But beware: If you withdraw early, you'll have to pay a penalty—often three to six months of interest.

Money Market With this type of plan, the bank pays you higher interest than a traditional savings account. You also can write two to three checks per month against a money market account.

Money Market Mutual Fund In this scenario, a mutual fund company invests your savings in short-term bonds, such as T-bills and CDs. Although this is an extremely secure option, these funds are not insured. This means that the mutal fund company will try to keep the value at $1 per share, but there are no guarantees. It is similar to a bank money market account, but it pays slightly more because it is not insured.

U.S. Treasury Securities These come in three major types: T-bills, T-notes, and T-bonds. How do they differ? Mostly in terms of how much you can invest and for how long. You can only buy T-bills, for instance, in minimum denominations of $10,000, and they have the shortest maturities (up to one year). T-notes are sold in 2- to 10-year maturities. The minimum investment amount for these is $5,000. Because these investments don't offer high returns, they're often used as a safe place to park money that you will need in the near future.

U.S. Government Series EE Bonds These are commonly known as savings bonds. You buy these bonds for half their face value, which can be $50 or $75. You can buy up to $10,000 worth. When you cash in the bond at maturity (generally 12-17 years, depending on the interest rate), the bond will be worth the amount stated on the face of the bond. People frequently buy these types of bonds as gifts for young children.

ASK THE EXPERTS

I recently put my emergency money in a one-year CD. I was laid off last week and need it now. Can I withdraw the money?

Yes, you can withdraw your money from the CD, but you will have to pay a penalty for withdrawing it before it matures. The penalty depends on your bank: Some charge three months' interest, others six months'. In the future, consider putting your emergency funds in a money market account, since those accounts do not have penalties for withdrawals.

Where can I find the best rate on CDs?

You can start by checking out **www.bankrate.com**, which compares CDs by rate or by state. You can also read up on CD rate trends and get FAQs about CDs. Another place to check is your local credit union.

automatic investment plans

Put your savings on autopilot

Don't have the time, energy, or discipline to put your money away in all these different kinds of investments? Relax. You can make it easy by signing up for an **automatic investment plan**. These plans automatically deduct the amount you want saved each month from your paycheck or checking account, so you don't have to worry about disciplining yourself to save; the plan does it for you. Most people don't really miss money saved in this way because they never see it—and you can't be tempted to spend money you don't see! Here are two of your options:

Workplace retirement program When saving for retirement, contributing to your company's 401(k) plan or some other tax-deferred account is too good a deal to pass up. Your savings automatically come out of your paycheck in pretax dollars, which your employer invests for you in a tax-deferred account; this is usually a mutual fund you select from a range your employer offers you. You pay no taxes on the money saved or the interest or gains earned from it until you withdraw the money at retirement.

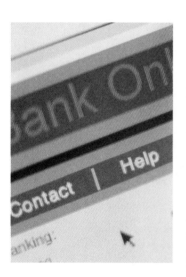

Many employers will also match a portion of the funds you put aside, such as 25 or 50 cents on the dollar, up to a certain amount. (Think about that: Very few banks or mutual fund companies offer a 25 or 50% return on your money!)

Automatic withdrawals from your checking account Most mutual fund companies also offer automatic savings plans. Let's say you want to plunk $100 into a fund each month to save for a new house in 10 years. Simple. The amount can be automatically deducted each month—just as your 401(k) contributions are—except it comes out of your checking account instead of your paycheck. Unlike a 401(k) contribution, however, this money is not a pretax contribution.

When you enroll in an automatic investment plan, financial institutions may waive their minimum investment requirements, allowing you to get started with as little as $50. Banks offer similar programs, and you can also buy U.S Savings Bonds this way.

ASK THE  EXPERTS

How can I find out more about my company's retirement plan?

Company retirement plans are such a hot issue that most firms have really boosted their efforts to get the word out to employees. You should have no trouble finding plenty of consumer-friendly information at your workplace about signing up for your firm's 401(k) plan (plus information about matching dollars and other provisions, too). The best starting place may be the human resources department. Ask about a 401(k) informational Web site, a 401(k) employee newsletter, and/or 401(k) planning workshops or seminars. Many companies offer employees one or more of these educational resources.

I'd like to save up for a car. How do I arrange to have money automatically withdrawn from my checking account each month?

Just about everybody plays the automatic savings game these days. Simply call up the bank, brokerage, or credit union in which you want to plunk your savings and ask for an application for an automatic investment plan. Once you receive the form, you'll have to decide how much money you want to have withdrawn from your checking account each month, which type of investment you want your money put into, and what day of the month you want the money withdrawn. Your investment choices will range from money market accounts to stocks, savings bonds, and mutual funds, depending on the financial institution that you contact. The withdrawal date will depend largely on when you get paid; most people pick the 1st or the 15th of the month. All of this will be even easier to do if your paycheck is automatically deposited into your checking account; otherwise, you will have to make sure to deposit your paycheck before the withdrawal date. Then, sit back—and watch the savings pile up.

basic investing

Balancing risk against return

Good for you. By sticking to your budget, you've managed to squirrel away substantial savings in safe investments. Now you're ready to consider some riskier investment options, which have the potential to bring you much higher returns. All you need is an investment that will give you a good yield, which is a bit easier said than done.

You can start by asking yourself these two important questions:

1. What kind of **return** are you looking for? Return is how much money you want your investment to make over time.

2. How much **risk** are you willing to take? Risk is the possibility that an investment will not perform to expectation.

As a rule, the higher the investment risk, the higher the investment's potential return. For example, stocks, or ownership stakes in public companies, go up and down in value. That fluctuation in price means you can lose money if you have to cash in your stocks when prices are down. However, you are generally rewarded over the long term with higher returns than you would get on a risk-free investment, such as a savings account or a CD.

How much risk can you handle? To some degree it's about individual comfort level. Some people are risk averse, or avoid risk at all costs. Others jump in headfirst without worrying about the consequences. But circumstances, such as your age, how much time you have to meet your investment goal, how much extra money you have on hand, the size of your portfolio (e.g., your investable assets), your income, and the security of your job, should be factored into your willingness—or unwillingness—to take risks. Younger people can typically tolerate more risk because they have more time to recoup any losses if their investments decrease.

Finally, don't overlook the sleep-at-night factor. If you're not sleeping at night because you're worrying about your investments, then sell them. Pick a less risky investment.

Time is on your side

Investors often talk about a time horizon. That's the number of years (or months) that you have to invest your money before you need it. If you're saving for your eight-year-old son's college education, for example, you have a time horizon of 10 years. This number is important because your time horizon dictates (to a large extent) the types of investments that you should select.

Generally, the less time you have, the more conservative you should be. And the more time you have, the more aggressive you can be. Why? More aggressive investments, such as stocks, have the potential to earn higher returns than conservative investments like certificates of deposit (CDs). However, aggressive investments fluctuate wildly in value, whereas conservative investments don't. If you need your investment money in one year's time to buy a car, for example, you can't take the risk that stock prices may be down. But if you won't need the money for many years, you can afford to take a bit more risk because you will be able to wait out a market downturn and cash in your investment when the market is up again.

FIRST-PERSON DISASTER STORY

Basket case

Fifteen years ago I started working for a small, successful company that had great benefits, including a 401(k) plan. The 401(k) offered three or four mutual funds to choose from, as well as a fund of company stock. Because the fund of company stock had the highest return, I put all my money in that one. At first this seemed like a great idea, because within a year or two the company was growing like wildfire. To take advantage of the growth spurt, I also decided to invest in company stock. Over the next several years, my 401(k) expanded exponentially, and the stock price just kept going up. Three years ago, however, the CEO resigned and the company hired a new one. After that, the stock price dropped dramatically. At that point, I should have changed my 401(k) allocation, but I didn't. I really did think things would improve eventually. However, they only got worse. The stock is now worth just a quarter of what it was when I bought it. Now I'm about ready to retire, and my 401(k) is worth about as much as it was when I started 17 years ago, plus I lost all that money I invested in company stock. My father always said not to put all my eggs in one basket. I wish I had listened to him.

—Bradley S., San Jose, CA

stocks

Grab a piece of a company's financial pie

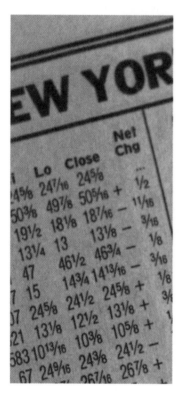

If you're eager to get even bigger returns on your investments, it's time to consider the stock market. But be careful! Those opportunities for higher returns can come at a price.

Here's how it works: If a company wants to raise money to expand its business, it can go public. What this means is that the owners offer investors the opportunity to buy into the company by purchasing shares of stock, thereby becoming part owners. After a company goes public, it is listed on the stock exchange and its stock can be traded (bought and sold) by the public. If the company wants to raise more money, it can issue more stock.

There are different stock exchanges, and the exchange on which a company is listed is determined by the size of the company and the size of the offering. As a company becomes more profitable and its earnings rise, its stock price should also increase, as well as the dividends it pays to investors. (A dividend is like a cash bonus, and its amount is determined by the company's board of directors at quarterly meetings.) Some growth companies don't pay dividends, but this doesn't make them bad to invest in.

If we lived in a perfect world, every listed company would be profitable, stock prices would always be on the rise, and you would never have to worry about losing your money. However, the price of a stock can be negatively impacted by many things: fluctuations of the dollar overseas, changes in interest rates, amendments to the tax code, rising or falling inflation, changes in production, increased competition, and so on.

This is why it is so important to choose stocks carefully. Not only do you need to know what to buy and sell—you also need to know when to do it. This is where an investment advisor can be a great help. A good advisor will match your tolerance for risk with your investing goals and create a portfolio containing the right combination of low-, medium-, and high-risk stocks to help you reach those goals.

ASK THE  EXPERTS

I'm afraid of losing my money. What are the safest stocks to invest in?

In general, buying stock in major utility and manufacturing companies is usually safer than investing in growth stocks. Because the price of these stocks does not rise and fall very much, they tend to offer reliable dividends. Investing in these kinds of stable megacorporations, or so-called "Dogs of the Dow," might be a good option for people with low risk tolerance—and who are willing to let their stocks slowly accumulate value over time. Learn more about the Dogs of the Dow investing strategy at **www.dogsofthedow.com**.

What's the best way to learn if a stock is a good investment?

You can start by learning about the company and its performance over the last 5 to 10 years. Look for this important information:

Dividends If a company pays dividends, consider it worthy if the dividends have risen over the last 10 years.

Annual earnings Solid companies will show increased earnings in at least 5 out of the last 10 years.

The stock's price-to-earnings (P/E) ratio This ratio reflects the price of one share of stock divided by the company's net earnings during the past four quarters. As of May 2003, the P/E for Standard and Poor's 500 Index is 25. Anything over that means investors think the company is growing very fast and is positioned to make a lot of money. But it can also mean that the stock is just plain overpriced.

You'll find these details in Value Line's and Standard & Poor's reputable stock guides. These two top stock-rating firms track all the major stocks and offer succinct analysis.

bonds

**Making money
on interest**

Another way to try to earn bigger returns on your investments is to purchase bonds. A bond is a small loan that you make to a larger corporation or government through a financial institution such as Smith Barney or Merrill Lynch.

When a company or government needs a major loan, it will sometimes approach these financial institutions, which will give it a big chunk of change. The institutions then split this loan into a lot of little loans, beginning at $1,000 or $10,000 each, which they resell to investors as bonds. Bonds are like regular loans in that the company promises to repay you the money owed (called the principal) on a certain date (the maturity date). In the meantime, the company will pay you interest on the loan you made to them through the financial institution. You'll receive a check containing your interest earnings twice a year throughout the lifetime of the bond.

What's great about bonds is that on the maturity date, presuming the company has not gone bankrupt, you will get your entire loan back, called the face or par value of the bond. However, that does not mean bonds are without risks. If interest rates rise, the value of your bond will drop. For example, let's say you've been receiving checks for 6% interest on your bond. Then, inflation hits and interest rates go up to 7%, 8%, even 9%. However, your check doesn't change. You will still collect 6%, while it seems that everyone else is making more on their investments. If you want to sell your bond to get out of this situation, you'll have to sell it for a bit less than its original value in order to find a buyer.

ASK THE EXPERTS

My friend swears by bonds. Then all of a sudden she had to sell some and lost some money. What happened?

If your friend had to sell her bond before it matured and she lost money on the sale, it was probably due to a rise in the interest rate. In other words, if your friend wanted to sell a 6% bond when market rates on similar bonds were at 7% or 8%, she would have had to sell it at less than face value, because no investor would have wanted to buy her bond for what she paid for it. That's because that investor could buy a new bond paying higher interest. If, however, interest rates had fallen below 6%, then her bond would have been a lot more appealing and she could have sold it for more than she paid for it, because investors would want to have her bond's higher interest payments.

Is it true that some kinds of bonds are tax free?

Yes. You do not have to pay federal tax on the interest you earn from municipal bonds, though you may have to pay state income tax on them, unless they were issued by your state of residence. The federal government made municipal bonds tax free to encourage people to invest in public projects, such as schools and airports. Because of this benefit, municipal bonds usually pay less interest than corporate bonds.

What does it mean if the bonds I invested in are called?

If a bond is called, it means the borrower is paying back the bond sooner than the agreed bond maturity date. This usually happens when interest rates go down and the borrower wants to get rid of high-interest-rate bonds so it can issue bonds with a lower interest rate. Most bonds have an initial time period during which they cannot be called in, which is usually 5 to 10 years after they have been issued. If your bond is called after this period, there is nothing you can do—except start looking around for other bonds to invest in.

mutual funds

The investor's smorgasbord

Buying into a mutual fund takes a lot of the guesswork out of investing. Here's how it works: A portfolio fund manager and a team of investment experts pick and choose among dozens, hundreds, even thousands of stocks, bonds, and other financial instruments, looking for top performers to invest in. Then, they sell shares of their entire fund to investors like you, so you do not have to put money in each individual investment.

As more people invest in a fund, more investments can be added and the total assets rise. The greater the assets, the more power the

fund has in the market. And because the risk is spread over so many different kinds of investments, if a single stock nosedives or a particular bond is called in, the blow is softened by the hundreds of other investments.

If this sounds like a good deal to you, then you should start looking into mutual funds. As you consider different funds, check out their long-term performance; you want a mutual fund that shows a steady return over the years.

You can assess this performance by delving into the fund's scorecard. The **prospectus** lists the fund's objectives, holdings, and fees. Most of the important things you need to know are on the first few pages. The annual report, on the other hand, contains performance information. Look for a solid total return: This is the amount the fund earned from dividends and capital appreciation, minus expenses and fees. Also evaluate the volatility and risk of the stock versus its return. At sites like **www.morningstar.com**, you can compare funds and see which ones consistently perform well in their peer group.

One caveat: If you do want to buy into a fund, make sure the portfolio manager who made this fund so successful is still with the fund when you do so.

ASK THE EXPERTS

I want to invest in a mutual fund, but I don't have enough cash to meet the minimum requirement. Now what?

Although many funds require a minimum investment, some companies will waive this if you open an IRA account (Individual Retirement Account, see page 180) or agree to have at least $50 automatically withdrawn from your bank account every month and deposited into the fund. This is an easy way to build up your investment without panicking about whether you're buying in at the right time. Buying monthly also ensures that you buy more shares when the fund is cheap and fewer when they are more expensive. This is called dollar cost averaging and it's a wise investment strategy. If you invest in a fund this way, however, hang on to your monthly statements; the tax consequences of selling your shares later can get tricky.

How do I track the price of my mutual fund?

Look in the financial section of your daily newspaper for your fund's Net Asset Value, or NAV, or check Yahoo finance (**http://finance.yahoo.com**). The NAV is the value of all the stocks and bonds owned by the fund, divided by the number of the fund's shares owned by its investors. If, for example, your fund has $5 billion worth of stocks, bonds, and other investments, and investors own 500 million shares of the fund, then your fund's NAV would be $10. This would be the price of a share in this fund. However, keep in mind that your fund's NAV may change as the prices of stocks and bonds increase or decrease.

Will I have to pay a commission to buy into a mutual fund?

It depends on the fund. Some charge a commission and others don't. Funds that charge commissions, called load funds, can be bought from a stockbroker, some investment advisors, or from the fund company itself. Some load funds hit you with a redemption fee if you sell your shares early; most funds prefer that you stay with them for at least five years. There are also funds with a back-end load, which means you pay a fee when you sell, as well as a variety of no-load funds. With no-load funds, you don't have to pay a commission to the middleman because you buy shares directly from the fund. However, you may be charged about .25% in annual fees to cover distribution, marketing, and sales of the fund, so read the **prospectus** carefully.

diversification

**Keeping yourself
well covered
with a variety
of investments**

Congratulations! You've mastered your budget and the savings are starting to pile up. And you're probably eager to start increasing those savings by playing the investing game.

But before you run right out and put all your hard-won money into high-risk stocks or bonds, you should know that financial experts recommend **diversification**. That means don't plunk all of your money into one investment, no matter how lucrative it promises to be. Instead, you should spread your risk around by investing in a variety of options. This way, if one investment sours, such as a stock, you won't lose as much as you would if your entire portfolio was invested in that stock. The bottom line? Don't put all your eggs in one basket.

As your savings grow, a financial planner (see page 24) can help you best decide how to spread your money across different types of investments to ensure the highest return—at a risk level that does not give you nightmares.

From that point on, it should be pretty smooth sailing. Of course, you will need to monitor and adjust your investments over time, but the hardest part is over: You have reined in your expenses. You have created a budget, freed up some cash, and now you're socking that cash away toward your future goals. You have successfully planted your own personal money tree, and with a little TLC, that tree will keep on blooming for years to come.

Diversification strategies

Take a good look at these examples of diversification to get a feel for risk and return. Generally, the more you have in stocks, the greater your risk. What you need to ask yourself is how well you can weather the good and bad years—both financially and emotionally.

Low risk, low return
Best year return: 22%
Worst year return: -5%

20% money markets
50% bonds
30% stocks

Medium risk, medium return
Best year return: 26%
Worst year return: -14%

20% money markets
30% bonds
50% stocks

High risk, high return
Best year return: 30%
Worst year return: -18%

10% money markets
20% bonds
70% stocks

Investing over time

If you put $3,000 in a savings account that pays 1% interest, you will earn a little over $30 in a year. But what if you put it in a different investment—one that delivers a higher return? Look at what could happen to that money over the years:

	Mutual fund (3%)	Money market (5.5%)	Stock fund (12%)
1 year	3,091	3,169	3,380
3 years	3,282	3,537	4,292
10 years	4,048	5,193	9,901
15 years	4,702	6,833	17,987
20 years	5,462	8,990	32,678
30 years	7,371	15,562	107,849

now what do I do?
Answers to common questions

Should I start a savings plan if I'm in debt?

It depends on your particular situation. For some folks, it may be smarter to use any extra cash to pay down debt (and avoid paying more interest) rather than saving it. For other folks, though, it may make sense to start a savings plan—especially if the money that would have gone into savings is not used to pay off debt but is simply used to make more discretionary purchases. Finally, don't forget the psychological dynamic at work here. Many people feel helpless about their inability to save. Putting money into a savings plan often makes people feel that they're in control. If you're in debt, you can keep plunking some money into a savings plan as long it doesn't put you deeper into debt.

I have so many different financial goals. Do I need a different savings plan for each goal?

Yes—and no. Long-term goals, such as retirement and college tuition, generally need their own savings plans because there are different types of savings structures and tax consequences for each of these goals. A 401(k) plan, for example, is a tax-exempt plan for retirement savings, whereas a state 529 plan allows tax-exempt savings for education expenses. For shorter-term goals, such as saving for a car or a family vacation, one account will do, unless having separate accounts for each goal helps you focus.

Altogether, my various investments pay about 3% interest, and inflation is running about 3% each year. Does that mean I'm just breaking even?

That's precisely the problem. You want your money to "earn" more money over time, not just retain its original value. What's more, inflation is not fixed at 3%. It can—and does—run higher. At that point, you'd be losing money, and your hard-earned money would be worth less than its original value. Not to mention, at just 3%, you would probably be losing ground on taxes, too.

I've often heard that the earlier you start saving, the less you need to save. What does that mean exactly?

One way that your money grows over time is through a process called compounding. Compounding lets you earn interest on your interest. (You also earn interest on your original investment, of course.) Therefore, the longer that you let an investment "compound," the more your savings will grow—even if you don't add any more money to the account. And the more growth that your savings produce on their own, the fewer dollars that you'll actually have to save.

What's the difference between a bear market and a bull market?

A bear market is when stock prices are declining, while a bull market is when stock prices are increasing. These descriptions arose from the observation that when a bull strikes, he butts upward with his horns. A bear, on the other hand, swipes down with his paws.

Now where do I go?

Books

Your Money or Your Life: Transforming Your Relationship With Money and Achieving Financial Independence
by Joe Dominguez and Vicki Robin
Offers advice on how to assess your attitudes about money and control your finances.

Live Long and Profit
by Kay R. Shirley, Ph.D., CFP
Explains wealth-building strategies for every stage of your life. Includes dozens of good examples. If you're concerned primarily with retirement savings, check out another book by Shirley: _The Baby Boomer Financial Wake-up Call._

Contacts

To learn more about the types of investments available—and how to pick 'em—check out these personal finance Web sites:

- www.morningstar.com
- www.quicken.com
- www.smartmoney.com
- www.investoreducation.org
- www.aaii.org (the site of the American Association of Individual Investors)

glossary

Annual Statements Year-end statements issued by banks and credit card companies that summarize your account's activity—deposits and withdrawals, for example, or purchases and payments. Usually issued in December.

Assets Items that you own, such as your house and its contents, your car, and stocks.

Automatic investment plan A plan you set up with your bank that automatically deducts a set amont of money from your paycheck or checking account each month, depositing it into the savings account of your choice.

Bankruptcy A federal proceeding that legally freezes your debt payment obligations while you either work out a repayment schedule with your creditors or petition a court to cancel your debt. Individuals may file two types of bankruptcy: Chapter 7 or Chapter 13.

Beneficiaries The people who get the proceeds from your investments when you die.

Budget A financial plan that will help you keep track of your money, make smarter spending decisions, and get and stay out of debt.

Calculator Aside from the traditional adding machine, a high-speed number cruncher offered free on many Web sites to help you figure out complex numbers, such as how much money you need to save for your children's college education and for your retirement.

Cash flow analysis The relationship between what you earn and what you spend. To figure this amount out, simply subtract your expenses from your income.

Chapter 7 bankruptcy A type of bankruptcy filing that wipes out most debts by liquidating your assets and distributing the cash among your creditors. Most remaining debts are canceled. This is the most severe form of bankruptcy because it means selling nearly everything of value that you own.

Chapter 13 bankruptcy A type of bankruptcy that is for people with steady incomes who could pay off their debts if they had more time. Chapter 13 doesn't wipe out your debt: It reorganizes it. Under this arrangement, you don't sell your assets. Instead, you pay back your debts on a two- to five-year schedule arranged by a court-appointed trustee.

Commission-based planners Financial planners who do not charge directly for their advice. Instead, they earn a commission if you invest money through them in a stock, a mutual fund, or another investment.

Credit rating A rating attached to your credit report. The higher your rating, the better your credit and the easier it will be for you to request and get more credit (loans, credit cards, etc.).

Credit report A public record of your debts and payment history. Includes how much money you have borrowed, if you've ever missed a payment, and whether you have ever filed for bankruptcy.

Debt consolidation loan A lump sum of money you borrow from a bank that you can use to pay off your credit cards and other high-interest debts.

Discretionary expenses Expenses that don't occur on a regular basis and are generally for nonessential items. Example: movie tickets.

Disposable income The money you have left—after taxes are withdrawn—from your salary and any other sources of income, such as a stock that pays dividends.

Diversification Spreading your investment risk around by putting your money in different types of investments.

Emergency fund A cash reserve of roughly three to six months' income, set aside for emergencies and kept separate from other savings.

Equity line of credit A line of credit that you can take out from the bank by using your home as collateral.

Fee-only planners Financial planners who are paid for their advice—period. They may recommend that you buy certain investments, but they will never earn a commission for selling you a particular stock or mutual fund.

Financial goals What you want to spend your money on. A specific financial goal, complete with a price tag and the savings commitment you'll make each month, will help guide your spending and saving efforts.

Financial planner A money consultant who can advise you about everything from drawing up a budget and getting out of debt to saving for retirement or college tuition. See also fee-only planners and commission-based planners.

Fixed expenses Expenses that are the same from one month to the next. Example: your mortgage or rent payment.

Grace period The number of days you have until you are charged interest on your credit card purchases. The usual grace period is at least 25 days. If you carry a balance from one month to the next, however, you generally forfeit the grace period.

Gross salary The total amount that you earn before taxes, health insurance premiums, and other items are deducted from your salary.

Home equity line of credit A loan that you take out against your house. For example, you might take out a second mortgage for up to 80% of your home's current value, minus the balance on your mortgage. Once the paperwork is filed, the bank hands you a checkbook. When you need money, you can write yourself a check (up to the determined amount).

Inflation The annual rise in the cost of goods and services, measured in percentage points over the cost for the same item a year before.

Liabilities Debts that you owe, such as a mortgage and the unpaid balance on your credit card. Liabilities also include any spousal or child support you pay and any money you owe the IRS.

Liquidity How easily an asset can be converted into cash. Example: Money in a savings account is very liquid, because you can withdraw it immediately, while a long-term CD is not as liquid because you must wait years to cash it in.

Long-term financial goals Goals that take years and years—more than 10 years, in many cases—to achieve. Example: funding a retirement nest egg.

Market value The current dollar value of your possessions and the amount you would get, for example, if you cashed in your retirement plan or sold your house.

Medium-term financial goals Goals that you generally are able to accomplish within five years. Example: saving up the down payment for a home.

Microsoft Money One of the most popular personal-finance software programs. It lets you set up a personalized expense tracking system and also transfer information about your online banking transactions directly to your budget.

Minimum payment The minimum amount you must pay on your monthly credit card bill. Typically, this amount is based on a percentage of your total balance.

Negative cash flow When you spend more than you earn.

Net salary The amount you "net," or take home, after taxes, health insurance premiums, and other items are deducted from your salary.

Net worth A measurement of your current financial health. In simplest terms, it's what you own, such as your house, car, and stocks (known as assets), minus what you owe, such as your mortgage, car loan, and credit card debt (known as liabilities). Your net worth can be a negative or positive number.

Positive cash flow When you earn more than you spend.

Quicken A popular personal-finance software program. Just like Microsoft Money, it lets you set up a personalized expense tracking system and transfer information about your online banking transactions directly to your budget.

Refinancing Replacing your existing mortgage with a new, lower interest-rate mortgage.

Return How much your investment earns for you over time.

Risk How comfortable you are with the possibility that an investment will not perform up to your expectations.

Rule of 72 A calculation that tells you how fast your savings will grow. You do this by dividing 72 by the interest rate on your account. The answer is the number of years it will take for your money to double.

Second mortgage A house loan that works much like a first mortgage, except you usually take out a second mortgage if you need to free up some cash or want to lower your monthly mortgage payment or interest rate.

Short-term financial goals Goals that generally require immediate attention and are accomplished within a year or two. Example: saving up for a vacation.

Spending plan A financial plan to help you make the most of your money. In other words, a budget—but without the negative connotation.

Take-home pay The money you have left from your salary after taxes are withdrawn.

Time horizon The number of years or months that you have left to invest your money before you need it. Generally, the shorter your time horizon, the more conservative you should be with your choice of investment.

Unemployment benefits "Temporary income" that you can collect from the government for several months if you get laid off or fired from your job. The amount you receive depends on your former salary.

Variable expenses Expenses that you pay regularly, but which vary in the amount you pay each month. Example: groceries.

index

Y

about the author

Barbara Wagner has written about savings plans, investment strategies, and the dreaded B-word in over 50 articles. Her work has appeared in national magazines such as *BusinessWeek*, *Working Mother*, *Self*, and *First for Women*. She is also the author of six consumer finance books, including *Retiring*, a Barnes & Noble Basics book.

Barbara J. Morgan Publisher, Silver Lining Books

Barnes & Noble Basics
Barb Chintz Editorial Director
Leonard Vigliarolo Design Director

Barnes & Noble Basics™ *Personal Budgeting*
Wynn Madrigal Senior Editor
Barbara Rietschel Art Director
Jennifer Pellet Editor
Emily Seese Editorial Assistant
Della R. Mancuso Production Manager

Silver Lining Books would like to thank the following consultants for their help in preparing this book: Sheryl Garrett, CFP™, Founder of the Garrett Planning Network, a nationwide network of fee-only, hourly financial advisors headquartered in Shawnee, Kansas (www.garrettplanningnetwork.com); and Glenda Moehlenpah, CPA, CFP™ at Financial Bridges in San Diego, California (www.financialbridges.com).